Lewis Albert Sayre

The Alleged Malpractice Suit of Walsh vs. Sayre

Lewis Albert Sayre

The Alleged Malpractice Suit of Walsh vs. Sayre

ISBN/EAN: 9783337090203

Printed in Europe, USA, Canada, Australia, Japan

Cover: Foto ©Suzi / pixelio.de

More available books at **www.hansebooks.com**

MALPRACTICE SUIT

OF

WALSH *vs.* SAYRE.

New York:
GEO. H. SHAW & CO.,
LAW PRINTERS,
No. 176 Fulton Street.
1870.

INTRODUCTION.

As many members of the medical and legal professions, for whose benefit this is published, are so constantly occupied as to find little time to wade through the tedious details of the following trial, I have thought it best to give a short narrative of the facts of the case, and the results of it, that it may be understood without trouble.

On the 2d of April, 1868, while examining a patient in my private office, in the presence of Dr. Neftel, of this city, Dr. S. W. Gross, of Philadelphia, and several other professional gentlemen, Dr. Paine, my then assistant, brought in a poor woman with a child about 7 years old, which had a large swelling in the left glutral region. Detecting fluctuation in the swelling, I pronounced it a chronic abscess, probably connected with diseased bone, either of the sacrum, illium, or possibly the lumbar vertibrae, but that we could better tell its origin after we had emptied the abscess, and explored it, to its source.

There was a doubt expressed by some of the gentlemen present as to the accuracy of my diagnosis, and to prove its correct-ness, before opening the abscess I passed in an exploring needle, and pus following the withdrawal of the stylete, of course settled the question. On withdrawing the canula, I inserted a bistoury at the same opening and made an incision of half or three quarters of an inch, when the pus spurted out in a full stream, striking on the office floor, some distance from the child. The flow was suddenly checked by a large slough which filled the opening. This was pulled at with forceps quite strongly, and not being able to extract it, I enlarged the incision slightly, and its removal was followed by another gush of pus, of which *more than a pint* was caught in a basin, independent of what had been lost on the floor. This pus was mixed with a number of sloughs of cellular and connective tissue—one of which was considerably larger than a black walnut—and was the piece removed with forceps after the incision had been enlarged.

The mother became very much excited when I pulled out the slough above described, and she saw the pus spurting out from the wound. Seizing the child in her arms, she rushed around the office in a frantic manner, and it was with great difficulty that we could keep her still long enough to apply some solution of carbolic acid to the wound, and adjust a bandage. I requested her to return on the following morning, that I might ascertain the *cause* of the abscess, and thus be able to put the child upon some proper plan of treatment for its removal. This she promised to do as she left the office, but did not keep her promise, and I never heard from the child again until I was served with a notice of a suit for malpractice, in which I was charged with having punctured the hip-joint. As the child was the best possible—in fact, perfectly conclusive—evidence that this charge was false, I insisted upon bringing it into Court for the purpose of personal inspection. The child was brought into Court, but Mr. Edwin James, her counsel, objected to the *personal inspection* as a "*personal trespass*"—and would only permit an *oral examination*, which, in a child of only 7 years, was, of course, useless. The Court sustained Mr. James, as there was no precedent allowing *personal inspection* previous to the trial of the cause. Satisfied that the principle was correct, and if there was no precedent, it was time to make one, I petitioned the equity side of the Court to grant me this privilege, and Judge Jones, after a most exhaustive study of the subject, rendered an opinion which will make his name immortal, and confer such a protection against injustice to members of the medical profession, that I almost feel compensated for my own personal annoyance and expense, by being able thus to confer such a boon upon my profession.

It is easy to see that in a city like New York, where the legal calendar is very large, that a case may remain upon the docket many months, or even years, without being brought to trial. In the meantime, the patient who makes the charge may die, or be killed, and thus your principle witness for defence would be lost. In my case it did not make so much difference, as several witnesses were present; but suppose no one had been present, I should have opened the abscess just the same. Of course the scar would be my only witness, as to the place of puncture, and, of course, were the patient to die, or be killed before the case was tried, I should be subject to the mercy of perjured witnesses without the shadow of defence.

Take another case: A man charges a doctor with cutting off his big toe, and comes into court with twenty witnesses who swear they saw the doctor do it. The doctor has no evidence in defence, except the man's own foot, which, could it be uncovered of boot and stocking, would prove conclusively, that the charge was false, and at the same time show the necessity of a personal inspection. This has always been granted on the trial of the cause; but, as in my case, the trial may not be reached for months, or even years, after the charge is made. In the meantime your professional reputation is injured by the public dissemination of the slander, and in case of the death of the patient before the trial of the cause, your only evidence for defence is gone forever, although the heirs of the plaintiff will inherit the suit, which now you will have no means of defending.

In the trial of this cause the Court appointed a stenographer, Mr. W. E. Ruttan, who has taken an accurate report of all the proceedings, and I now publish them, at the urgent request of many members of the medical and legal professions, who have called upon me personally in relation to the matter, and also at the written request of two of America's ablest surgeons,—Drs. Gross and Crosby,—whose letters are hereunto annexed.

If the publication of this case shall have a tendency to put a stop to such vexatious suits, I shall be somewhat compensated for the annoyance to which I have been subjected.

LEWIS A. SAYRE.

285 Fifth Avenue, July 1st, 1870.

CONGRATULATORY LETTERS.

PHILADELPHIA, June 17th, 1870.

My Dear Doctor,—I sincerely congratulate you upon the successful issue of the villainous suit against you for alleged malpractice. A few more such verdicts will go far in putting a stop to such outrageous and unjustifiable prosecutions. It is only to be regretted that the persons who instigate them cannot also be made to suffer. You have achieved a great triumph, in which every honorable professional man in the country will sincerely rejoice with you. I hope you will publish a full account of the case, not only as a matter of sheer justice to yourself, as an able and accomplished surgeon, but for the gratification of your professional brethren, and for the instruction of the American bar—some of the members of which are, unfortunately, too prone, for the sake of a paltry fee, or a little ephemeral notoriety, to encourage and engage in such prosecutions. It has always appeared to me that a lawyer who will permit himself to bring suit for malpractice against an honorable medical man, known and recognized as such by the community in which he lives, must be essentially a base, unprincipled man, and I have no doubt that this would be found to be the fact if access could be had to the records of our courts, and their professional history ascertained. The few exceptions that would be found would only serve to prove the rule.

Again urging you to place all the facts in the case before the profession, I am, dear doctor, very truly your friend,

S. D. GROSS.

To Prof. LEWIS A. SAYRE, M.D., New York.

8

DARTMOUTH MEDICAL COLLEGE,
HANOVER, N. H., July 2d, 1860.

Prof. LEWIS A. SAYRE: *My Dear Sir,*—I take the liberty of addressing you at this time, to offer you my hearty congratulations on the result of the recent suit instigated against you for malpractice.

Your triumphant vindication is not only a source of gratification to your numerous friends, but is an actual benefit conferred upon the profession whose battle you have fought while defending your own reputation from assault. If the simple opening of an abscess is to render a surgeon liable to a suit of this character, the practice of surgery becomes too expensive a luxury for men of moderate means to indulge in. The result in your case showed conclusively that the public do not propose to assassinate surgeons in any such way. I am impressed with the fact that this suit has established some legal points of the highest importance to the profession. It is worth the while to know that a Court can, and will order an examination of the patient by a board of unprejudiced surgical experts *at the time the case comes into court.* It is even more satisfactory to know that a groundless suit, instigated by malice, cannot be undertaken with impunity, but that the plaintiff, as in your case, may be properly punished by the infliction of extra and unusual costs upon him by the Court. If our Courts could go a step farther and inflict any well merited punishment on the persons who instigated such suits, we should be well advanced toward the millenium of surgery. I am glad to know that you have passed so triumphantly through this annoying ordeal. Will you not now publish the evidence in your case, and thus bring to the knowledge of the profession and the public the valuable points made in the trial of the suit.

Trusting that you may do this as a labor of love to the profession, if for no other reason, I am with great respect, your friend and servant,

DIXI CROSBY.

Superior Court,

CITY OF NEW YORK.

MARGARET SARAH WALSH, an infant, by
JOHN F. WALSH, her guardian,

        Plaintiff,

    against

    LEWIS A. SAYRE,

        Defendant.

Summons—
    For Relief.

To the Defendant, Lewis A. Sayre:

You are hereby summoned and required to answer the complaint in this action, of which a copy is herewith served upon you, and to serve a copy of your answer to the said complaint on the subscriber at his office, No. 229 Broadway, New York City, within twenty days after the service hereof, exclusive of the day of such service; and if you fail to answer the complaint within the time aforesaid, the plaintiff in this action will apply to the Court for the relief demanded in the complaint.

Dated August 21st, 1868.

        EDWIN JAMES,
           Plaintiff's Attorney.

SUPERIOR COURT, CITY OF NEW YORK.

MARGARET SARAH WALSH, an infant, by
JOHN F. WALSH, her guardian,

against

LEWIS A. SAYRE.

The above-named plaintiff, by Edwin James, her attorney,
states to the Court:

I. That the plaintiff is an infant, under the age of twenty-one
years.

II. That on the 27th day of June, 1868, upon application
duly made on that behalf, the said John F. Walsh was, by an
order of this Court, duly appointed the guardian of the plaintiff for the purposes of this action.

III. That the defendant is and holds himself out to be a surgeon, practicing in the City of New York.

IV. That the plaintiff, on or about the 10th day of March,
1868, was taken by her mother to the defendant, he being such
surgeon, as aforesaid, to be treated by him for a swelling and
injury in the neighborhood of one of her hips, and the cause of
which injury was unknown to the mother of the plaintiff, and
the defendant, in his capacity of such surgeon, was then consulted by and on behalf of the plaintiff, and was employed, and
then undertook such employment as a surgeon to heal and cure
the plaintiff.

V. That the defendant then made some operation upon the
plaintiff, against the strong protest of her mother, and so negligently and unskillfully conducted himself in the premises, and
with such want of care and skill as a surgeon, that, in attempt-
ing and making such operation, he punctured the joint of the
plaintiff, and then so carelessly cut and operated upon her that

the synovial fluid, which lubricates the cartilagenous surface of the said joint, then escaped and was let out by such unskillful and negligent operation by the defendant, and the hip was seriously and permanently injured.

VI. That by reason of such want of proper skill and negligence, all on the part of the defendant, the plaintiff was made sick, and her system seriously affected, and the said joint, and the whole leg rendered useless and permanently lame, and that the plaintiff is now in such a condition that it may be necessary to amputate her leg, at the risk of her life, or she may remain permanently injured and disabled.

VII. That the plaintiff has sustained injury to the extent of $20,000.

Wherefore the plaintiff demands judgment against the defendant for the sum of twenty thousand dollars damages, together with costs of this suit and such other or further relief as may be just.   EDWIN JAMES, Att'y for Pl'tiff.

City and County of New York, *ss.* :

John F. Walsh, being duly sworn, says :

That he is the guardian, *ad litem*, in the above entitled action, duly appointed by this Court, as stated in the foregoing complaint.

That he has read the foregoing complaint, and knows the contents thereof, and that the same is true of his own knowledge, except as to the matters therein stated upon information and belief, and as to those matters he believes it to be true.

And he further says that the plaintiff herein is an infant of the age of seven years and no more, and that her enfeebled physical condition and her extreme youth, render her incapable of taking an oath, which, with this deponent's personal knowledge of the allegations in the complaint made, are the reasons why this affidavit was not made by the plaintiff.

J. F. WALSH.

Sworn to before me, this }
  21st day of August, 1868. }
      C. A. L. GOLDEY, Notary Public,
            N. Y. City and County.

NEW YORK SUPERIOR COURT.

MARGARET SARAH WALSH, an infant, by
JOHN F. WALSH, her guardian,

against

LEWIS A. SAYRE.

The defendant, for his answer to the plaintiff's complaint in the above entitled action, alleges :

First. That he has no knowledge or information sufficient to form a belief, except from the complaint herein as to whether, upon application duly made, the said John F. Walsh was duly appointed guardian of the plaintiff for the purposes of this action, and therefore he denies the same.

Second. This defendant admits that he is a surgeon, practicing in the City of New York.

Third. This defendant further admits that on or about the 10th day of March, 1868, the plaintiff was brought to him by her mother to be treated by this defendant, in his capacity as a surgeon, at his office, No. 285 Fifth Avenue. That this defendant, upon careful examination, found the said Margaret Sarah Walsh, the plaintiff, to be suffering from an abscess on her body, near one of her hips, which this defendant, as such surgeon, operated upon in a careful and skillful manner, and then immediately thereafter carefully and skillfully bandaged and dressed the affected part, and this defendant denies the allegations in the 5th and 6th sections of said complaint contained, to wit: that he negligently and unskillfully, and with want of care and skill, performed such operation.

And this defendant further denies that he negligently, carelessly or unskillfully or otherwise punctured any joint of the said Margaret Sarah Walsh, or injured her hip, or that he so negligently, carelessly or unskillfully cut and operated upon her, that by reason thereof she became sick or permanently lame, or that by reason of negligence and want of proper skill on the part of this defendant, he in any way or manner permanently or otherwise injured her or her hip, or the joint thereof, or any joint of said plaintiff, or caused the synovial fluid thereof to escape, as in the said sections of said complaint alleged, and this defendant alleges that all the allegations in that respect in said complaint contained are false and untrue.

And this defendant further denies that said Margaret Sarah Walsh, the plaintiff, by reason of want of care and skill on the part of this defendant in making said operation, has sustained any injury in any way or manner, or in any sum whatever. And this defendant further denies each and every allegation in said complaint contained, except those allegations herein before specifically denied or expressly admitted.

And this defendant, for a further and separate defence to the said pretended cause of action, alleges that such operation was performed by him with great care and skill, and with and according to the best professional judgment, knowledge, and skill of this defendant.

And this defendant, for a further and separate defence to the said pretended cause of action in said complaint set forth, alleges and charges the fact to be, that the said plaintiff, and the mother and father of the said Margaret Sarah Walsh, were the direct cause of and contributed to whatever injury that may have come to the said plaintiff since such operation, by reason of their negligence and want of proper care thereafter, by willfully and negligently, and against the advice, consent and instructions of this defendant and his assistants, given to the said mother at the time such operation was performed, in abruptly taking the said Margaret Sarah Walsh away from this defendant's office, and not returning there with her for further treatment, and care and attention, by this defendant, as her physician and surgeon, as expressly and particularly directed and requested so to do by this defendant and his assistants at the time such operation was performed as aforesaid, and contrary to this defendant's request and desire, and his frequent attempts to do so, he has never since been allowed by her parents to see or attend the said Margaret Sarah Walsh, the plaintiff. Wherefore this defendant demands judgment against the plaintiff, that the said complaint may be dismissed with costs.

P. J. GAGE & BRO.,

Def't's Atty's.

City and County of New York, *ss. :*

Lewis A. Sayre, the defendant herein, being duly sworn, deposes and says that the foregoing answer is true to his own knowledge, except as to the matters therein stated on information and belief, and as to those matters he believes it to be true.

LEWIS A. SAYRE.

Sworn to before me, this }
7th day of September, 1868. }

W. S. GERRISH, Notary Public,

City and County of N. Y.

NEW YORK SUPERIOR COURT.

MARGARET SARAH WALSH, an infant, by
JOHN F. WALSH, her guardian,

against

LEWIS A. SAYRE,

City and County of New York, *ss.:*

Morris Wolf, being duly sworn, deposes and says, that at No. 534 Washington Street, in the City of New York, on the 12th day of September, 1868, he served upon John F. Walsh, personally, copies of the annexed notice, affidavit and summons for the examination of the said Margaret Sarah Walsh, the plaintiff herein, by leaving the same with the said John F. Walsh, and at the same time and place exhibiting to him the within originals; and that he knew the said John F. Walsh to be the individual mentioned and described in said notice, affidavit and summons as guardian of the said Margaret Sarah Walsh.

MORRIS WOLF.

Sworn to before me, this 14th
  day of September, 1868.

HALE KINGSLEY, Notary Public,
County of New York.

NEW YORK SUPERIOR COURT.

MARGARET SARAH WALSH, an infant, by
JOHN F. WALSH, her guardian,

against

LEWIS A. SAYRE.

City and County of New York, *ss.:*

Wellesley W. Gage, being duly sworn, deposes and says, that at No. 121 Charlton Street, in the City of New York, on the 10th day of September, 1868, he served upon Margaret Sarah Walsh personally, copies of the annexed notice, affidavit and summons for the examination of the said Margaret Sarah Walsh, the plaintiff herein, by delivering to and leaving the same with the said Margaret Sarah Walsh, and at the same time and place exhibiting to her the within originals, and also delivering to and leaving with her the sum of fifty cents, being the necessary fees as required by law for her attendance as such witness as aforesaid; and that he knew the said Margaret Sarah Walsh to be the individual mentioned and described in said notice, affidavit and summons.

WELLESLEY W. GAGE.

Sworn to before me, this 11th
day of September, 1868.

WILLIAM T. GRAFF, Notary Public,
City and County of New York.

NEW YORK SUPERIOR COURT.

MARGARET SARAH WALSH, an infant, by
JOHN F. WALSH, her guardian,

against

LEWIS A. SAYRE.

To the above-named plaintiff, Margaret Sarah Walsh :

We hereby give you notice that we require you to personally appear and attend before one of the Justices of the said Superior Court, at the Chambers of said Court, corner of Chambers and Centre Streets, in the City of New York, on the 22d day of September, 1868, at 12 o'clock, noon of that day, to be examined as a witness on the part of the defendant, pursuant to the provisions of the Code of Procedure for such purpose and to the provisions of the Statute entitled of taking testimony conditionally within this State, and that if you refuse or neglect so to appear and attend, we shall then and there apply to the Court for such relief against you as is provided for by said code.

Dated New York, September 9th, 1868.

P. J. GAGE & BRO.,
Def't's Attorneys.

NEW YORK SUPERIOR COURT.

MARGARET SARAH WALSH, an infant, by
JOHN F. WALSH, her guardian,

Plaintiff,

against

LEWIS A. SAYRE,

Defendant.

City and County of New York, *ss.:*

Lewis A. Sayre, of said city and county, being duly sworn, deposes and says :

That he is the defendant in the above entitled cause. That on or about the 21st day of August, 1868, an action was commenced in said Court against this deponent by the plaintiff in the above entitled cause, by the service of a summons and complaint. That said action is now at issue. That said action is for the recovery of damages as alleged in said complaint to have been caused by negligence and want of proper care and skill on the part of this deponent as a surgeon in an operation performed by this deponent as such surgeon on the plaintiff, Margaret Sarah Walsh. That said damages are laid in said complaint at the sum of twenty thousand dollars. That since the commencement of said action the said plaintiff has been absent from said city. That this deponent has sought an interview with said plaintiff for the purpose of obtaining a professional examination by this deponent and other surgeons of the parts of the plaintiff so operated upon as aforesaid. That this deponent has been refused such interview and examination as aforesaid. That immediately after the operation upon said plaintiff as aforesaid, the mother of said plaintiff took her away from the office of this deponent and refused to, and has not returned with said plaintiff nor allowed said plaintiff to be returned to this deponent for further treatment, as requested by this deponent and the assistant of this deponent. That neither this deponent nor the assistant of this deponent has been allowed to see said plaintiff since the operation as aforesaid. That it is requisite and necessary for the proper defence of said action, that the plaintiff in said action be required to appear and be examined as a witness. That said plaintiff is placed beyond the reach of this deponent and the guardian of said plaintiff absolutely refuses this deponent the privilege of such examination. That said action cannot be properly defended, nor this defendant cannot safely proceed to the trial thereof without such examination being first had as aforesaid.

LEWIS A. SAYRE.

Sworn to before me, this 8th
   day of September, 1868.

     W. S. Gerrish, Notary Public,
         City and County of New York.

NEW YORK SUPERIOR COURT.

Margaret Sarah Walsh, an infant, by
   John F. Walsh, her guardian,

        against

     Lewis A. Sayre.

To the above-named plaintiff, Margaret Sarah Walsh:

Upon reading the affidavit of Lewis A. Sayre, the defendant, hereto annexed, and the pleadings in the above-entitled action, you are hereby summoned and required to personally appear and attend before me, one of the justices of the said Superior Court, at the Chambers thereof, to be held at the court-rooms thereof, corner of Chambers and Centre streets, in the City of New York, on the 22d day of September, 1868, at 12 o'clock noon of that day, to be examined as a witness in the above-entitled action, for and at the instance of the defendant above-named, pursuant to sections 390 and 391 of the Code of Procedure, and to the provisions of the Statute entitled "of taking testimony conditionally within this State," and in case of your refusal or failure to appear, attend and testify, you will be liable to be punished as for a contempt of court, and your complaint may be stricken out.

Witness—The Hon. Samuel Jones, one of the Justices of said Court, at the court-rooms thereof, at the City of New York, on the 9th day of September, 1868.

S. JONES, Justice.

The plaintiff having appeared to the within summons, the further hearing under the within summons is hereby adjourned to September 24, 1868, at 12 M.

New York, September 22d, 1868.

S. JONES, Justice.

The plaintiff having appeared to the within summons the further hearing thereunder is hereby adjourned by order of the Court to October 1st, 1868, at 12 M.

New York, September 24th, 1868.

S. JONES, Justice.

The plaintiff appeared to the within summons, pursuant to adjournment, and the further hearing under the summons herein is hereby adjourned by consent to October 8th, 1868, at 10 A. M.

New York, October 1st, 1868.

S. JONES, Justice.

The plaintiff appeared, and the further proceedings under the within summons is hereby adjourned by consent to October 13th, 1868, at 10 A. M.

New York, October 8th, 1868.

S. JONES, Justice.

NEW YORK SUPERIOR COURT.

Margaret Sarah Walsh, an infant, by
John F. Walsh, her guardian,
against
Lewis A. Sayre.

The following testimony of the plaintiff was taken before the trial, pursuant to the foregoing summons :

The plaintiff appeared pursuant to the annexed summons and adjournments, this 13th day of October, 1868, and being duly sworn by Justice Robertson, testified as follows :

My name is Margaret Sarah Walsh ; I am six, going on seven years of age ; I live at 121 Charlton Street, in this city ; I have brothers and sisters ; I have one sister older, Mary Kate Walsh ; I have a sister younger, her name is Teressa Walsh ; I don't know the months of the year ; I know when it is Winter and when it is Summer ; I know when it is warm weather and when it is cold weather ; I remember going to Dr. Sayre's office with my mother ; she took me there ; it was in cold weather ; I was there once before with Dr. Vaughan ; I don't know when it was ; when I went there with my mother I went into the room down stairs ; I went up stairs and saw Dr. Sayre ; no gentlemen went up stairs with us ; Dr. Sayre then examined me, and said I had no spinal disease, and no hip disease, and then took a big probe and probed this side (putting her hand on her left side), and took a big knife and began to cut me ; I don't know what next he did ; I don't know how long he was cutting me ; there were five gentlemen present, they were doctors ; they were talking about my case when he examined me as to what it was ; I know where the mark is, it is on the left hip, it is plain to be seen with my clothes off ; it is not running or discharging now ; there was no mark or cut there before the doctor probed or cut me ; I never went back there afterwards; after I left Dr. Sayre's office Dr. Vaughan came up the same day to our house; I don't know whether he has been my father's doctor as long as I can remember or not; Dr. Parker and Dr. Carnochan saw me afterwards; I went to Dr. Parker's house; I don't know where he lives; Dr. Vaughan, my father and mother went with me; I don't know how many days after Dr. Vaughan called; it was before we went to Dr. Parker's; I think it was about a month when we went to Dr. Parker's; Dr. Carnochan was not there; he did not come there; yesterday we went to Dr. Parker's, and he was in the country, and we went to Dr. Carnochan's; Dr. Parker never was at our house; we were twice at Dr. Parker's house; I know what twice means; I don't know whether we were there more than two times; I forgot how many times we were at Dr. Carnochan's house.

Q. Maggie, I desire to have the Doctors examine the place that Dr. Sayre cut.

Mr. James, counsel for plaintiff, objects.

Objection sustained by the Court.

When I went to Dr. Parker's he did not probe me or cut me; he looked at my leg; Dr. Carnochan did not probe or cut me; he did not hurt me; Dr. Parker, Carnochan or Vaughan, did not probe or cut; Dr. Tucker I have seen; he was at our house; I don't know when it was; he never saw me but once; I have never seen any other doctors than those I have mentioned; Dr. Vaughan tends to me now, and has been at our place almost every day; Dr. Vaughan never probed me or cut me; it don't hurt me to walk; it don't hurt me much; there is a pain where the sore is; there is a pain in the back (witness pointing to the small of the back), I have had no instrument on my leg to support it; only a bandage.

her
MARGARET × SARAH WALSH.
mark.

Sworn to before me, this }
   13th day of October, 1868. }

ANTHONY L. ROBERTSON,
Ch. J. Superior Court, New York.

SUPERIOR COURT.

MARGARET SARAH WALSH, an infant, by
   JOHN F. WALSH, her guardian,

       against

    LEWIS A. SAYRE.

We hereby mutually consent that the filing of the within testimony of Margaret Sarah Walsh, the plaintiff, be, and the same is hereby waived, that the same be treated as having been regularly filed, and that the same may be read upon the trial of the above entitled cause, in evidence, by either party, with the like effect, as though the same had been regularly filed with the Clerk of said Court.

Dated New York, November 10th, 1868.

        P. J. GAGE & BRO., Atty's for Def't.

        EDWIN JAMES, Att'y for Pl'ff.

The following testimony was taken before trial, under summons granted by the Court:

The plaintiff, John F. Walsh, appeared, pursuant to the annexed summons and notice, and, being duly sworn by the Hon. A. L. Robertson, Chief Justice, the 13th day of October, 1868, testified as follows:

I am the father of Margaret Sarah Walsh; she is going on seven years of age; she was born the 10th of February, 1862; she has resided with me since, except when she was in the country this summer; I don't know the date when she left or when she returned to the city; she was gone seven or eight weeks, to New Jersey, Fort Washington, and Rockaway; she was with a nurse; she was with Mary Bowers as her nurse, who lives in Charlton Street; don't know the number.

The plaintiff's examination herein is hereby adjourned, by consent, to October 15th, 1868, at 12 M.

New York, October 13th, 1868.

J. F. WALSH,
P. J. GAGE.

Ordered accordingly,
A. L. R.

The examination of John F. Walsh continued October 15th, 1868 :

I have learned since that Mary Bowers lives at 113 or 11^5 Charlton Street; I think I have seen her since I was last examined, but I am not positive : she ceased to have charge of my child when we returned from Rockaway, the last of August or beginning of September, 1868; we were in the habit of visiting Rockaway before this summer, but not the summer previous; the visit to Rockaway, Fort Washington, and New Jersey helped the child; her health is pretty good now; I don't understand what you mean in regard to health; I mean by health that one feels well in their system, but I don't mean by health whether they have pains or not; Dr. Vaughan, Dr. Parker and Carnochan have charge of her now; I have incurred, I suppose, between five and seven hundred dollars in expenses in regard to the child; I swear in the complaint that I only spent $500, and don't know why I did not claim more; I have paid Carnochan $30 or $40, I don't know which; I have no bill or receipt for it; I have paid Parker about $15.

Q. What did you pay Dr. Tucker ?

A. I don't remember; I think I have not paid him anything.

Q. Has he rendered you a bill ?

A. I have almost forgotten.

Q. Do you remember his rendering you a bill ?

A. I think I do ; of about ten dollars.

Q. What were your expenses in New Jersey?

A. About thirty dollars.

Q. How much in Rockaway?

A. About two hundred dollars.

Q. Have you charged it all or in part?

A. I don't think I charged it all; I can't tell you how much, or in what proportion; I remember that when I went to my lawyer I reckoned it over in my own mind; I reckoned about $150 or $200 to Rockaway, $150 to Vaughan, about $30 for New Jersey, and $185 for expenses elsewhere; I believe that I reckoned that in, but I don't remember what else I reckoned in; I put in Parker's and Carnochan's $35 or $40.

Q That makes $610 so far?

A. No, sir; I don't add in Tucker's.

Q. You have already shown that you have run up the expenses to $610; how do you claim, then, only $500?

A. I wanted to be as light as possible in the bill.

Q. You think Dr. Vaughan went to New Jersey?

A. I don't know of his being there.

Q. Was he at Fort Washington?

A. Yes, sir.

Q. How far is this from New York?

A. I believe about from eight to ten miles from here.

Q. How many times did Dr. Vaughan go there?

A. I don't know; don't know as he went at all; he did not go with me.

Q. Did you ever take this child to Dr. Sayre's?

A. No, sir; I did not.

Q. Did you ever go with the child when taken there, or to anybody else?

A. No, sir; but I remember it, she was taken to Dr. Sayre's in March; I cannot say that the child was sick at all; I noticed that there was a lameness about her, but she did not complain of pain.

Q. What did she complain of?

A. I never heard her complain at all.

Q. What was she taken to Dr. Sayre's for?

A. Because of her lameness.

Q. It was not a subject of conversation in your family that something was the matter of her?

A. No, sir.

Q. How long before that it was consulted in your family that something was the matter of her?

A. I do not know; I believe that Dr. Sayre was a better doctor than any other; I did not notice a swelling; she appeared well in every way, excepting an inclination to lameness; she did not complain of pain; I do not remember that it was a subject of talk in my family at any time.

Q. Did you see her after she was brought back from Dr. Sayre's?

A. Yes, sir; it was in March; I did not examine her person after she was brought back.

Q. Was she taken anywhere excepting to her own house?

A. No, sir.

Q. When was she taken away from your house?

A. When she was taken to Fort Washington.

Q. Did she go to any doctors?

A. She was taken to Dr. Parker's; I went with her; I think she had been to Dr. Parker's before I went with her.

Q. What is your occupation?

A. I am a ship-carpenter; I am not at home all the time during the day: I am certain that she has not been to any doctor after coming from Dr. Sayre's; Dr. Vaughan went with me to Dr. Parker's; Dr. Vaughan has been my family physician for several years.

Q. What did he call it?

A. I think he said it was rheumatism, or something like rheumatism; he did not call it a disease; I did not hear her say anything about it.

Q. How long was it that she went to Dr. Parker, after having been to Dr. Sayre?

A. I do not know; think it was about two months.

Q. Did Dr. Parker probe her?

'A. No, sir; he made an inspection or examination; I do not

know how long he was engaged, perhaps half an hour; he took off her clothes; I did not tell him where she had been until after he had examined her.

Q. What did you then tell him?

A. I told him that Dr. Sayre had operated upon her.

Q. Did she tell him that Dr. Sayre had cut her?

A. I disremember what she said, except that he had performed an operation.

Q. What did Dr. Parker say?

(Objected to and exception taken.)

A. He said that the joints had been opened and the synovial fluid had been let out; I do not remember any more; he told the doctors to give her something nourishing; I think iron water, I cannot tell; they held a consultation.

Q. Was any local applications or instruments used?

A. I did not see him use any; there were splints applied to the hips by Dr. Vaughan, through the direction of other doctors; he did it the day after coming from Dr. Parker's; I cannot tell you the month; it was in September when we went to Dr. Parker's; I think I had not been to Fort Washington before this.

Q. When was the operation performed by Dr. Sayre?

A. In March, I think; I know the weather was rough and cold; it was summer when we went to Fort Washington and to Dr. Parker; between that and the other time nobody had charge of her but Dr. Vaughan.

Q. Did Dr. Tucker have anything to do with her?

A. I do not know whether he had or not.

Q. Were you at Dr. Parker's more than once?

A. I was there a short time after the first time; it might have been a week; the examining parties then called; Dr. Parker examined her again; he took off her clothes.

Q. What did he say to you?

(Objected to.)

A. He did not tell me anything; I think I was in the room;

I do not remember what I heard him say; I did not hear what was the matter with her; he talked about the treatment of her.

Q. Report what he said the time of your first visit.

A. He said the joint had been opened and the fluid let out; he said it was opened in an operation; this is the way, I think, that I understood it.

Q. Don't you know?

A. I speak as far as I know; I don't know whether I have any doubt; I want to speak the truth; I have no doubt, as to my remembrance, that was it in substance.

Q. The second time you went there, did he make an operation?

A. No, sir.

Q. When did you go again?

A. I can't tell you; it may have been within a month.

Q. Do you keep books?

A. I keep books for my own business; but I did not make minutes of these things.

Q. Did you keep any minutes of expenses you paid out?

A. No, sir; not when I paid bills; I did to liquor bills, but not of grocery bills; I have no minutes of what I paid Dr. Parker; I paid him each time I paid him a visit; the first time it was about $5.00, and the same amount the second and third times.

Q. Did you go with the child to Dr. Parker the third time?

A. Yes, sir.

Q. What did he then say?

A. I think he said that the child was getting along well and was better; he said nothing about the difficulty; I did not propose it in any way.

Q. Did he ever make a statement in writing?

A. Not that I know of; I never asked him to; he never gave me a statement to my lawyer; I never asked him to go down to my lawyers.

Q. When was the fourth time of your visit?

A. A few days ago; I did not see him; I do not know the interval that had elapsed.

Q. Do you know what this month is?

A. Yes, sir.

Q. Don't you know when you went to Fort Washington?

A. I don't know whether it was September or October when the child returned; I think it was September, about the beginning of it or the middle; I did not see him; I have told you all I know about it.

Q. When did you go to Dr. Carnochan's?

A. I cannot tell; it was after going to Dr. Parker's the first time; he came to the house; Dr. Vaughan fetched him there, I think, after I had been to Dr. Parker's; Dr. Parker was not there at the time; I was there when the doctor came; it was at the middle of the day; I came to see the doctor; I think that Dr. Parker knew that Dr. Carnochan was coming.

Q. Did Drs. Parker and Carnochan ever see her together?

A. No, sir; Dr. Carnochan examined her; I think it was a couple of days after coming from Dr. Parker's.

Q. What did he say?

(Objected to and exception taken.)

A. He said that the joint had been opened and the fluid let out.

Q. How did he say it was opened?

A. I do not remember what he said; I think he said the hip-joint had been opened and the fluid had run out; he did not say whether it had been done by disease or operation.

Q. What did Dr. Parker say as to that?

A. He said it was done by operation.

Q. Will you swear that Dr. Parker said it had been done by operation?

A. I swear that, to the best of my knowledge, he did.

Q. Did Dr. Carnochan probe it?

A. He did not, and he did not say that it was done by disease or operation; they put us out of the room.

Q. When were the splints put on?

A. I do not know if there had been splints on before or after Dr. Parker's inspection.

Q. Did Dr. Carnochan ever give you a statement in writing?

A. No, sir.

Q. Did he advise you to commence this suit?

A. No, sir.

Q. Did Dr. Parker?

A. No, sir; I never knew them to advise me or anyone about the suit.

Q. Did Dr. Vaughan advise you?

(Objected to.)

A. I think he told me that Dr. Sayre was to blame for this.

Q. Did he advise you to sue him?

A. Not directly; he might have indirectly.

Q. Did Dr. Tucker ever advise you to sue him?

A. No, sir; I did not see Dr. Tucker when I was there.

Q. Have you told me all you heard Dr. Carnochan say when there?

A. Yes, sir.

Q. Did you tell Dr. Parker that Dr. Carnochan had seen her?

A. No, sir; but I think Dr. Vaughan did.

Q. Who went with her on her visits to the doctor?

A. The same parties went each time; he did not probe her; he only felt of her.

Q. What did he say the fourth time?

A. I heard him say that she was improving and getting along, etc.; I did not hear him say what was the matter.

Q. When were you there the third time?

A. It might have been two or three weeks since, I can't tell.

Q. Did he use any instrument?

A. No, sir.

Q. How much did you pay him?

A. $20 the first time and $5 the next.

Q. How many times were you at his house?

A. Three or four times.

Q. Did he probe the wound?

A. No, sir; I never knew that anybody probed it after Dr. Sayre did.

Q. Did any other doctor have charge of her than Drs. Parker, Carnochan, Tucker, and Vaughan?

A. No, sir; I should have known it if such had been the case.

Q. Who is Dr. Tucker?

A. I said Dr. Tucker might have seen her.

Q. If anybody else had attended her would you have known it?

A. I should have heard of it.

Q. Did the sore discharge or run?

A. Yes, sir.

Q. How long, and when after the sore had been examined by Dr. Parker and Dr. Carnochan did it stop running?

A. It stopped running after they had seen it?

Q. When?

A. Some three or four months; it has healed up and she is improving; but she is lame; she leans on one side and stands on her toe.

Q. Do you mean to swear that a casual observer would notice that she was lame to see her walk?

A. Yes, sir.

Q. Does she stand on one toe?

A. She leans mostly on the toes of the foot that is lame.

Q. Were you here the other day when the child was sworn?

A. Yes, sir.

Q. Was the child operated upon by Dr. Sayre the same—this child I have been examining you about?

A. Yes, sir; I say the child is lame.

Q. Does it walk straight?

A. I think it does not put the heels on the ground equally when it walks.

Q. Do you swear that she does not?

A. I will not swear to that; but that she leans most of her weight on her toes.

Q. When she stands still would it be noticed?

A. When she stands still she looks perfectly regular and natural.

Q. Do you think that one who had never seen her on seeing her walk in the Court room the other day would say she was lame ?

A. Yes, sir.

Q. Did you never hear her complain of her back ?

A. No, sir.

Q. Did you hear her complain of her back the other day when here ?

A. I did, sir.

Q. Did you not hear her swear ?

A. I heard her say it; that is, heard you tell her so.

Examination of John F. Walsh continued this 5th day of November, 1868:

Q. Did you ever see Dr. Sayre about the condition of the child, or the claim you make in this case before the commencement of this action by you or the child's action ?

A. I think I did not.

Q. Don't you know whether you did or not ?

A. I know I did not.

Q. Did you ever present a bill to him for the moneys you claim to recover ?

A. No, sir.

Q. Did you ever give him notice in any way or form that you intended to sue him ?

A. No, sir.

Q. Why didn't you give him notice or present your bill ?

A. The only reason I know is, I did not have any instructions from my counsel.

Q. Don't you present your bills when persons owe you without counsel's instructions ?

A. Why certainly.

Q. What explanation can you give for taking the child back, or making any claim of any character to Dr. Sayre before bringing suit ?

A. The explanation is, sir, Dr. Sayre was to send his own doctor to doctor the child in our house.

Q. Who says he agreed to do this?

A. My wife.

Q. You did not hear it?

A. No, sir; he did not send anybody.

Q. When he did not send anyone, why did you not send for him or take the child back?

A. The child would not go back; she screamed and hallowed when she heard his name mentioned.

Q. Was that the only reason why you did not take her back, or send for him.

A. Yes, sir.

Q. Did you or its mother try to coax her to go back?

A. I think the mother did, I am not quite positive; this is my best recollection.

Q. How is the little girl to-day?

A. I think she is improving; she walks better; it's general health is improving.

J. F. WALSH.

Sworn to before me, this 5th }
day of November, 1868. }

John M. Barbour.

We hereby mutually consent that the filing of the within testimony of John F. Walsh be, and the same is hereby waived; that the same be treated as having been regularly filed, and that the same may be read upon the trial of the above-entitled cause in evidence by either party with the like effect, as though it had been duly and regularly filed with the clerk of said Court.

Dated New York, November 10th, 1868.

P. J. GAGE & BRO., Att'ys for Def't.

EDWIN JAMES, Att'y for Pl'ff.

Unwilling to believe the testimony of Mr. Walsh, even under oath, in regard to Dr. Parker's complicity with this case, I called upon Dr. Parker with Dr. Paine, the evening after Mr. Walsh had given his evidence. The following statement of Dr. Paine, written the same evening of the visit, gives a very correct history of that interview:

November 21st, 9½ P. M., 1868.

On Saturday evening, November 21st, 1868, I called upon Dr. Willard Parker, at his residence in Twelfth street, in company with Dr. Lewis A. Sayre, for the purpose of ascertaining whether he had stated to Mr. Walsh that Dr. Sayre had punctured the hip-joint of Mr. Walsh's daughter, as testified to in the case of " Walsh vs. Sayre," for malpractice.

Dr. Parker at first denied that he had told Mr. Walsh that Dr. Sayre had punctured the hip-joint. He then said he would tell all he could remember about the case, " which was that the mother of the child and Dr. Vaughan came to his office and requested him to examine the child for some trouble about the hip ; that he measured the limbs and found no difference in length, pain on pressure of the joint, or difficulty in motion, and therefore he at once told them there was no hip disease. There was a small opening about the size of an ordinary probe, about midway between the trochanter major and the tube-ischia," from which was oozing a small quantity of synovial fluid. The mother stated that that was the place where you (Sayre) ran a long needle, and said you ran it in six times, a needle as long as this probe, (holding an ordinary pocket probe in his hand) and as I could not tell what you might have struck with it, I did not know whether you had punctured a bursæ or tendon, or possibly might have punctured the capsule of the hip-joint itself. I remarked, " Why, Dr. Parker, I was present at this operation, and there was nearly half a pint of pus escaped with a sudden gush on the floor, before I could get the basin to catch it, and a good deal flowed afterwards."

When Dr. Sayre asked him if he thought it possible to puncture a healthy hip-joint and have a permanent sinus from which there was a constant flow of synovial fluid, and that joint still remain perfectly healthy, as he said this one was ? Or whether it was possible to have this opening into the joint, without having positive and serious symptoms which could not be mistaken, and which, he stated, did not exist?

These questions Dr. Parker evaded, and said, "well, if you ran a six inch needle anywhere around there, here and there, as the mother said, why of course I could not tell what you might have done, or where your needle went to."

Dr. Sayre then said, "Well, Dr. Parker, I understand you to say, then, that you would take the statement of any ignorant Irish woman, of such an unnecessary and barbarous proceeding, as correct, rather than to trust to your knowledge of that surgeon's skill, to prove her story false."

Dr. Parker replied, "Well, I thought it very strange, and certainly that you did not know as much as I thought you did, if you went fishing around the hip-joint in the way they said you did."

Dr. Sayre replied, "Then you believed her statement, and never inquired of me to know if it were true, but on the strength of her assertion you told them I had punctured the hip-joint?"

Dr. Parker answered, "Of course we have to take the statements of patients as they give them to us. It is none of our business to go around and inquire whether they are true or not. I did not tell the mother that you had punctured the hip-joint, but I said to Dr. Vaughan, in the other room, that I thought you had punctured the capsular ligament, and that accounted for the synovial fluid, "as they told me there was no abscess, and nothing but blood came from all your cuts, of course I could not account for this synovial fluid in any other way. If they had told me of the abscess, of course I would have understood it; but I never heard of the abscess until to-night, and if I was to give my evidence now, according to the facts as given to me now, why, of course, it would be entirely different."

When asked about the law suit, he said he had heard something about it; he could not tell where, but it seemed to him that he had heard there was some trouble about it.

Dr. Sayre replied that Mr. Walsh swore in Court that he had brought the suit on Dr. Parker's testimony; he (Parker) said he believed he did say something about a law suit the second visit they made to him, and he told them he was sorry; he did not think they would make anything out of it. "That he had been sued once in the same way for an operation on a little girl's elbow, and had to pay Dick Busteed $300 to have it hushed up," and that he thought that was the same way;" the man merely sued you to make you pay up a little money, and so I gave myself no bother about it, as I thought you could fix that without any trouble, and thought that would be the end of it; but if I had thought there was going to be a *real suit, and have a regular trial, why I would have stopped it*, as I was able." Dr. Sayre replied : "Then I understand, Dr. Parker, that you would permit me to be sued for malpractice, in puncturing a healthy hip-joint, based on your testimony to the father—my professional reputation destroyed by the public announcement of the case, and you would make no objections to it as long as you thought that I would hush it up and never let it come to trial; but that if you had thought that it was going to come to trial, and your ignorance exposed upon the witness-stand, that then you would have stopped it. Good evening, sir; I think I now understand you," and we left. The above statement is a very fair description of the interview between Drs. Parker and Sayre, and most of the language used by them is verbatim and quoted accurately.

O. SPRAGUE PAINE, M.D.,
90 East Thirty-first Street.

NEW YORK SUPERIOR COURT.

MARGARET SARAH WALSH, an infant, by
JOHN F. WALSH, her guardian,

against

LEWIS A. SAYRE.

To the Honorable Superior Court of the City of New York :

The petition of Lewis A. Sayre, the above-named defendant, respectfully shows to the Court,

That he is the defendant in the above-entitled action and a surgeon, practising in the City of New York, and that the plaintiff is a child of the age of seven years, as your petitioner is informed and believes.

That this action was commenced on the 21st day of August, 1868, by the above-named plaintiff against your petitioner, for an alleged negligent and unskillful operation performed by your petitioner, as such surgeon, upon the body of the said plaintiff on or about the 10th day of March, 1868, and that the damages laid in said complaint is twenty thousand dollars.

That your petitioner did, on or about the day last named, operate upon the plaintiff, who was suffering from an abscess on her body near one of her hips.

That such operation was so performed by your petitioner ; that a large quantity of pus or matter was withdrawn from such affected part.

That immediately after such operation upon said plaintiff as aforesaid, the mother of said plaintiff took her away from the office of your petitioner, and has ever since wrongfully refused to return to your petitioner's office with her, and that the mother and father have not returned with her, nor allowed the said plaintiff to return, or be returned to your petitioner's office for further treatment, as expressly requested at the time of such operation by your petitioner and his assistant so to do.

That since the commencement of proceedings in this action, your petitioner and his assistants have gone frequently to the house of the plaintiff for the purpose of making and obtaining a professional examination of the affected part of the plaintiff so operated upon as aforesaid ; but neither your petitioner nor his assistants, although such request was expressly made to the parents of said plaintiff, have been permitted or allowed to see or examine, professionally and as her physician, the affected part so operated upon as aforesaid.

That your petitioner says that it is requisite and absolutely necessary for the proper defense of said action, and to properly protect his good name and fame in his profession, that the said plaintiff be required by this Honorable Court to appear and be examined as hereinafter prayed.

That the plaintiff, through her counsel, alleges that this action is based upon the certificates of surgeons of this city as to such injury.

That your petitioner hereby refers to the pleadings in this action and makes them a part of this his petition.

That said plaintiff is placed beyond the reach of your petitioner, and the guardian of said plaintiff, although requested, absolutely denies to your petitioner the right and privilege of seeing her, or to make such examination and personal inspection of the injured part of said plaintiff by your petitioner and other competent surgeons ; and that your petitioner cannot properly defend said action, and cannot safely proceed to the trial of the same, without such examination and such personal inspection being first had by your petitioner, and by such other eminent and skillful surgeons as may be deemed necessary by him for such defense.

Wherefore, your petitioner prays that such examination and

personal inspection of the plaintiff, and of the affected part, by
your petitioner, and by such other skillful and competent surgeons as he may name, under the direction of the Sheriff of the
City and County of New York, or of a referee for that purpose,
to be appointed with the usual powers of referees, which
appointment is hereby prayed for the purpose of conducting
such examination, and allowing your petitioner, and such other
surgeons to be named by him as aforesaid, to make such personal inspection of the plaintiff and of the affected part, whose
testimony in regard to the same he shall take, or that such
examination and personal inspection may be had at such time
and place, and in such other form or manner as to the Court
may seem just, and proper and that your petitioner may have
such other and further relief as to the Court may seem just and
equitable in the premises.

LEWIS A. SAYRE.

City and County of New York, *ss.:*

Lewis A. Sayre, the above-named defendant, being duly
sworn, deposes and says, that the foregoing petition is true of
his own knowledge, except as to the matters therein stated on
information and belief, and as to those matters he believes it to
be true.

LEWIS A. SAYRE.

Sworn to before me, this 2d
day of October, 1868.

W. S. Gerrish,
Notary Public,
City and County of New York.

NEW YORK SUPERIOR COURT.

MARGARET SARAH WALSH, an infant, by
JOHN F. WALSH, her guardian,

against

LEWIS A. SAYRE.

Upon the foregoing petition and the pleadings in this action, let the plaintiff, or her attorney, show cause before me, one of Justices of this Court, at the Special Term thereof, to be held at the Chambers thereof, in the City of New York, on the 6th day of October, 1868, at 10 o'clock in the forenoon, or as soon thereafter as counsel can be heard, why the prayer of the said petition should not be granted, and why the said petitioner should not have such other and further relief as the nature of the case demands, and as to the Court may seem just and proper in the premises.

Dated New York, October 3d, 1868.

S. JONES, Justice.

The following important opinion was rendered, and order made, on the foregoing application:

NEW YORK SUPERIOR COURT.

MARGARET SARAH WALSH, an infant, by JOHN F. WALSH, her guardian,

Plaintiff,

against

LEWIS A. SAYRE.

Defendant.

Heard Special Term, October, 1868.   Decided Nov. 12, 1868.

EDWIN JAMES for plaintiff; P. J. GAGE for defendant.

The action is brought against the defendant, who is a surgeon, to recover damages for an alleged unskillful operation performed by him on the body of the plaintiff, who is a child of about seven years of age.

The complaint alleges that the defendant was employed, in his capacity as surgeon, to treat the plaintiff for a swelling and injury in the neighborhood of one of her hips; that he performed an operation on the person of the plaintiff, but did it so negligently and unskillfully as to puncture the joint of the plaintiff, causing the synovial fluid which lubricates the cartilaginous surface of said joint to escape, thereby seriously and permanently injuring the hip, rendering the whole leg useless and permanently lame, and, perhaps, rendering necessary an amputation of the leg, at the risk of plaintiff's life.

Damages to the amount of $20,000 are asked for.

The defendant, by his answer, alleges that plaintiff was suffering from an abscess on her body near one of her hips, which he, about March 10, 1868, operated on in a careful and skillful manner, and immediately after the operation carefully and skillfully bandaged and dressed the affected part, and denies all the allegations of negligence and unskillfulness contained in the complaint; and then sets up that, whatever injury may have come to the plaintiff since said operation, it was caused by the negligence of the plaintiff and her parents in not returning the plaintiff to the defendant, as requested, for further medical treatment.

The defendant now, upon the complaint and answer, and upon a petition setting forth that this action was commenced August the 21st, 1868, that plaintiff is a child about seven years old; also, setting forth the substance of the contents of the complaint, and reiterating the matters contained in the answer; also, setting forth that plaintiff's counsel alleges that this action is based upon the certificates of surgeons as to the injury, that since the commencement of this action he and his assistants have endeavored to obtain leave to make a professional examination of the affected part of the plaintiff, but have been refused permission so to do by plaintiff's parents; that he verily believes that it is requisite and absolutely necessary, for the proper defence of this action, and to properly protect his good name and fame in his profession, that a personal inspection and professional examination of the affected parts should be had by him and such other eminent and skillful surgeons as he may deem necessary, and that, without such personal inspection and examination, he cannot properly defend this action, nor safely proceed to trial; and praying that said examination and personal inspection by him and such other skillful and eminent surgeons as he may name, may be had, under the direction of the Sheriff, or a referee appointed for that purpose, or at such time and place, and in such other form or manner as to the Court may seem just and proper; moves that the prayer of the petition be granted.

JONES, Justice—The question whether a surgical operation has been unskillfully performed or not is one of science, and is to be determined by the testimony of skillful surgeons as to their opinion, founded either wholly on an examination of the part operated, or partly on such examination and partly on information derived from the patient; or, partly on such examination, partly on such information, and partly on facts conceded or proved at the trial; or, partly on such examination and partly on facts conceded or proved at the trial.

The present action is brought on the faith of the expressed opinion of surgeons that the operation was unskillfully performed. This opinion is founded on the examination of the part operated on, and the natural presumption arising from the circumstances is that it is also founded in part on statements made by the patient and her parents. To what extent, if at all, the judgment of these surgeons in forming their opinions was influenced by a bias created, unconsciously to themselves, by such statements cannot now be determined. That must be left for the trial. It is, however, fair to assume on this motion the possibility of the judgment having been swerved by such bias.

As the determination of the action depends on the judgment of skilled surgeons, the defendant will prosecute his defence under serious, if not disastrous disadvantages, if this motion be denied. For, in that event, he will have to combat the testimony of those surgeons who have already formed their opinions adverse to him, possibly under the influence of an unconscious bias, and who have not only so formed it but expressed it, whereby, in the language of an eminent writer, "the expressed opinion has become as a fact to them who expressed it" (the meaning of which is that the mind of one who has expressed an opinion naturally exerts its utmost power and resources to sustain the opinion and refute all objections urged against it), by his own testimony alone, and that of his assistants present when the operation was performed, upon which testimony the usual criticism will, undoubtedly, be passed, viz.: As to himself, that he is a party in interest swearing to relieve himself from pecuniary responsibility and to preserve his reputation, and as to his assistants that they are not sufficiently skilled to have their testimony weigh against the plaintiff's witnesses.

There is no just reason why the defendant should be suffered to remain under this disadvantage when it can be easily avoided by a resort to the same means by which it was created.

While cases may occur where such ignorance or gross neglect is displayed that all competent surgeons would unite in condemning the operator, yet, in the present advanced state of surgical science cases frequently happen where surgeons of the greatest skill will differ with each other in their diagnosis of the nature and character of the difficulty to be remedied, in their views as to whether an operation would produce a cure ; as to whether it would be of some benefit to the patient, although not a radical cure ; as to whether the amount of benefit to be gained would justify the performance of an operation ; as to whether the operation could be performed at all without destruction of life, and, lastly, as to the best mode of performing the operation.

Of course it cannot now be ascertained to which class this case will ultimately be found to belong ; but on this motion, nothing appearing to the contrary, it must be assumed that the defendant has a fair prospect of succeeding in his defense, which cannot be if the action falls in the first class.

In a case, then, where skilled surgeons may honestly differ in their views, it is not proper that the cause should be left to be determined on the evidence of two or three surgeons selected by the plaintiff out of the whole body of surgeons, perhaps because their views are adverse to the defendant's ; but it is eminently proper that defendant should have the benefit of the testimony of one or two surgeons of his own selection, and that these surgeons should have the requisite means of forming a correct judgment, one of which is an examination of the affected part.

True, the plaintiff's witnesses may on the trial be examined as to the facts on which they formed their opinion, and may be called on to give a description of the part operated on, and it is suggested that upon the evidence thus given any number of surgeons whom the defendant pleases to call may found opinions.

I have, however, had sufficient experience in the trial of causes to know that witnesses, when giving a description, frequently honestly differ in material points.

This occurs sometimes by one fact or circumstance arresting the attention of one, while it escapes that of another, sometimes by an inaccurate measurement of distances either by the eye or instrument, more frequently, however, by the eye, and sometimes from a forgetfulness of some facts or circumstances which forgetfulness frequently arises in consequence of the facts or circumstances so forgotten not at the time of their occurrence striking the mind of the witness as material, and, therefore, making no impression on his memory, although they are, in fact, most material.

The evidence of the plaintiff's witnesses will be open to all these defects, while that of surgeons selected by the defendant, who have prosecut d their examination with light afforded by suggestions offered by him as to the line of examination proper to be pursued, will (although it may in itself be liable to similar defects) bring forth all facts and circumstances which exist and are deemed material by them or by the defendant. Thus, each party having an opportunity to investigate and ascertain as to existence of facts and circumstances deemed by each to be material, every fact and circumstance bearing in the least on the subject will be ascertained and spread forth in the evidence, whereby other medical witnesses will be the better enabled to form a correct judgment, and the jury be the better enabled to arrive at the truth.

If the Court has power on this application, to compel a discovery of the character of the one sought for, this is a proper case in which to exercise it.

Courts are instituted for the purpose of deciding disputes between litigants. To do this they must determine the truth of such material questions of fact, as are in controversy. In the performance of this duty, certain rules of evidence were established as being the best, that, without infringing on public policy, could be devised for the ascertainment of truth. It was, however, considered that individual should yield to public benefit. Therefore no rules of evidence, contrary to the interests of the public at large, could be adopted, although beneficial to individual litigants.

Among the rules thus established, were those that exclude a party from being a witness in his own favor, and also a person pecuniarily interested in the result of a litigation, from being a witness on behalf of the side on which he was so interested.

Two reasons were assigned for these rules; the one, danger of prejudice to the opposite party, by the introduction of false testimony by witnesses biased by such interest; the other, danger to public morals, by offering an inducement to perjury, and falsification of books and papers. Both these reasons spring from the interest of the party or witness who is offered as a witness.

There was a further rule which forbid a party to an action from being examined as a witness at the instance and in behalf of his adversary; and, as an incident of this further rule, a party was not allowed to obtain either an inspection before trial, or the production at the trial, of the books, papers or documents of his adversary.

This last rule is sometimes said to be founded on a general principle of law, that no man shall be compelled to give evidence against himself; but this principle is itself deduced from the same doctrine upon which the first two rules rest, since it is evident that bias and temptation to commit perjury and falsify is as strong to one who is compelled to give evidence against himself, as it is to one who voluntarily testifies in his own favor.

These rules were as ancient, as well settled and as firmly established as any of the principles of the Common Law.

But in course of time, the last of these rules was found to be such a drag on the ascertainment of truth in judicial investigations, as, in civil actions, to overbalance the objection to such compulsory examination and production, arising from apprehended danger to the public morals, and it was considered, that so far as prejudice to the party desiring the examination of his adversary was involved, it was matters for his own consideration, and if he chose to subject himself to that prejudice, it was not for the Court to interfere.

The country was ripe for a change.

The Judges of the Court of Common Law, however, deriving their power from, and proceeding, according to the course and principles of the Common Law, found themselves constrained to hold that they had no power or authority to set at naught, out of their own heads, by judicial decision, the well-settled principles of the Common Law above referred to, and therefore to hold that they had no power to compel the examination of, or the production of, his books, papers and documents, by one party, at the instance and in behalf of the other.

This want of power became an acknowledged defect in the administration of justice by Courts of Common Law.

Black. Com., vol. 3, pp. 381, 382.

In looking around to find the means to obviate this defect, attention was naturally directed to the Court of Chancery, which, in the causes whereof it then took cognizance, proceeded, according to the form of the civil law, upon the examination and oath of the parties, and which had withstood an attack made upon it by the Commons, for so proceeding against this form, and in subversion of the Common Law. (Black. Com., vol. 3, p. 52.) And it was conjectured that that Court, which had already interfered to mitigate the severity, or supply the defects in *judgments* at law, on the ground that it was against conscience to allow them to be enforced as originally rendered, would, on the same ground (it not being restrained by the above referred to principles of the Common Law,) compel a party to an action at law to make discovery of such matters as were necessary to be ascertained, to enable the Court of Common Law to determine the action according to the truth and justice of the case, since to conceal them would be contrary to conscience.

The experiment was tried and was successful.

It thus appears that the necessity of resorting to a Court of Chancery to obviate the defect in question, instead of having it remedied by the Courts of Law themselves, arose from the obstacle presented by the above referred to principles of the Common Law, and from that alone. But for these principles, Courts of Common Law, by their usual and ordinary process and proceeding—viz: by subpœna and rules of Court, both enforceable by attachment—could have met the requirements of the age, and supplied the defect. By subpœna they could have compelled the party to appear before the Jury, and there disclose those facts which were locked up in his breast, and by the same process could have required him to produce on the trial his books, &c., and by rule of Court (made upon parties over whose persons they had acquired jurisdiction, in an action of the subject matter of which they had jurisdiction), could compel him, before trial, to submit to an examination and also to produce his books, &c.

If, then, these principles of the Common Law have been abrogated by Statute Courts of Common Law, by virtue of their pre-existing and still existing Common Law powers, have full authority to compel a discovery upon the same principles, and to as full an extent and with as much completeness as the Court of Chancery was accustomed to do.

Of course, in exercising the authority, Courts of Common Law would look to the former decisions and principles of the Court of Chancery, and be guided by them, except where they were so manifestly unjust, unreasonable, or absurd as to justify their denomination as not law.

This presents two questions.

First. Have the above referred to principles of the Common Law been abrogated?

Second. Do the principles on which the Court of Chancery proceeded, in compelling a discovery, apply to and warrant the compulsion of a discovery of the nature, now asked for?

If both these questions are answered in the affirmative, the power of the Court to grant this motion is established.

The Legislature of the State of New York has enacted that in civil actions a party to the action may be examined as a witness, either in his own behalf or at the instance and on behalf of the adverse party; and, also, that no witness shall be excluded on account of interest.

These enactments abrogate (so far as civil actions are concerned) the common law principles that a party to an action or a person interested in the event shall not be permitted to give evidence in favor of himself, and that no man shall be compelled to give evidence against himself.

It may be urged that, as the enactment which abrogates these principles provides for discovery by the oral examination of a party, and by the compulsory production of his books, papers, and documents, it excludes all other discovery.

If the principles abolished by a statute are ones from which a Court derives authority to exercise certain functions, it would necessarily follow that the abolition of those principles abolished the authority, and then the only authority to act would be such as the statute gave.

But when the principles thus abolished had theretofore simply operated in restraint of the ordinary powers and procedure of a Court (which is the case here, as above reasoned), then abolition simply removes such restraint and leaves the Court to unfettered action, except in so far as it is curbed by provisions of the statute.

Thus, then, so far as a discovery by oral examination and production of books, papers and documents are concerned, the provisions of the statute are to be followed. But there is no prohibition against the compelling of any other discovery which may be conformable to the principle of the former practice of the Court of Chancery.

True, the Court of Chancery has been abolished, and it is enacted that no bill to obtain discovery under oath in aid of the prosecution or defence of another action shall be allowed ; but the principles of equity jurisprudence are still in force.

Courts of Equity, in compelling discovery, proceeded on the principle that it was against conscience that a party to a litigation having knowledge, or the means by which knowledge could be obtained, of facts material to the litigation, should obtain an advantage to himself to the sacrifice of the development of truth, and consequent working of injustice by withholding and concealing such knowledge and means.

Upon this principle a discovery of books, papers and documents is ordered.

The principle clearly covers and authorizes the compulsory discovery, in a proper case, of things or substances other than books, papers, etc.

It can readily be perceived that, although the cases would be rare where the discovery of any thing or substance other than books, etc., would be required or proper to be ordered, yet cases sometimes do occur (and this is one) where such discovery is both requisite and proper.

I am aware there is no recorded case of an application for any such discovery having been granted ; but, at the same time, there is no recorded case of any such application having been denied. It is probable no such application was ever made. The reason why it never was cannot be known, but many may be conjectured. Among them, that people are always timorous of taking the initiative, especially if the step is likely to subject them to large expense as a suit in Chancery would ; therefore, a case of urgent, almost absolute, necessity is requisite to set them in motion. It is probable that no case of sufficient urgency to overcome this timorousness occurred. Again at the time of the commencement of the action at law, the subject of which inspection is desired may either have been lost, destroyed, used up, or passed out of the control of the party, or have become so changed by natural or artificial causes, as that an inspection would be of no benefit. Again, as a suit in Chancery was of considerable duration, the subject would, in all probability, have become so changed from natural causes that an inspection, when ordered, would be of no avail. Again, in a large proportion of cases it may have been considered that the benefit to be derived would not be adequate to the expense.

A motion similar to the present obviates all these objections, except the second; for the principle being now established it will require but a few days to adjudicate on any particular motion, and the expense is but trifling.

Nor have I overlooked the fact that the Court of Chancery established many rules for its guidance in granting and refusing a discovery asked for; but none of these rules are antagonistic to granting this motion.

The fact that the discovery asked is of a portion of the body at first disposes the mind to regard it unfavorably, on the ground of delicacy. But it is not the first case in which such an examination has been had; as witness, Cases of Mayhem (Black. Coms., vol. 3, page 333); Cases of Divorce for Impotency (5 Paige Rep., 554; Beck's Med. Juris., vol. 1, pp. 116 to 125); Cases of Alleged Pregnancy (Beck's Med. Juris., pp. 204, 205).

Upon an examination, conducted under the authority of the Court there can be no undue exposure.

I conclude that the Court has the power on this application to order an examination, and that this a proper case in which to exercise it.

Motion granted.

At a Special Term of the Superior Court of the City of
New York, held at the Court Rooms thereof, at the
City of New York, on the 12th day of November,
1868.

Present : Hon. Samuel Jones, Justice.

NEW YORK SUPERIOR COURT.

Margaret Sarah Walsh, an infant, by
John F. Walsh, her guardian,

against

Lewis A. Sayre.

Upon reading and filing the petition of the above-named
defendant, wherein he prays the order or decree of this Court
that a personal inspection and examination may be had of
Margaret Sarah Walsh, the above-named plaintiff, and of the
affected part of her body, as alleged in her complaint herein,
by the said defendant Lewis A. Sayre, and by such other skillful and competent surgeons as he may name, etc., and upon
reading and filing the order to show cause granted upon said
petition, and the due proof of service of a copy of said petition,
and said order upon the attorney for the plaintiff herein, and
after hearing P. J. Gage, counsel for the defendant, in support
of such petition and application, and Edwin James, Esq., counsel for plaintiff in opposition thereto, now, on motion of said
defendant's attorney, it is hereby ordered that the following
named surgeons, to wit: Prof. Frank Hamilton, M.D., Ernest
Krackowizer, M.D., and William H. Van Buren, M.D., be, and
they are hereby permitted and allowed to make a personal surgical inspection and examination of the affected part of the
body of said plaintiff, before and under the direction of the
referee hereinafter named.

And it is hereby further ordered that John J. Townsend, Esq., counsellor at law, be, and he is hereby appointed referee, with the usual powers of referees as given by law, to conduct such personal surgical inspection and examination

And it is further ordered that defendant and his counsel may be present at such examination, but that no other persons shall be present, except such as plaintiff or her parents shall desire.

It is further ordered that said defendant, under the direction of said referee, may make such suggestions as to the line of examination as said referee shall deem proper.

And it is hereby further ordered that the said Margaret Sarah Walsh attend and appear before the said referee herein named at his residence, or at the residence or office of some one of the above-named three surgeons as he may designate, and on such days and at such hours as he may designate, and submit the affected part of her body to the inspection and examination to be made by the said surgeons above-named, and that said referee summon said plaintiff to attend and appear before him at such designated place, days, and hours, giving two days notice thereof, such summons to be served on plaintiff's attorney in the usual manner.

And it is further ordered that said plaintiff shall not be required to attend before said referee more than once, unless the referee shall deem further attendance necessary, in which case she may be required to attend twice more ; the attendances which shall prove abortive by reason of the plaintiff's fault not to be deemed as constituting a part of the three attendances hereby permitted to be required.

And it is further ordered that all proceedings on the part of the plaintiff and her attorney be, and the same are hereby stayed until she shall submit herself to such personal surgical inspection and examination so ordered as aforesaid, and until the said referee shall report the same to this Court.

(A Copy.)   JAMES M. SWEENY, Clerk.

THE SUPERIOR COURT OF THE CITY OF NEW YORK.

MARGARET SARAH WALSH, an infant, by
JOHN F. WALSH, her guardian,

against

LEWIS A. SAYRE.

To the Superior Court of the City of New York:

Pursuant to an order of the Court entered in this action, on the 12th day of November, A. D., 1868, whereby, among other things, it was ordered that the following named surgeons, to wit: Prof. Frank Hamilton, M.D., Ernest Krackowizer, M.D., and William H. Van Buren, M.D., be permitted and allowed to make a personal surgical inspection and examination of the affected part of the body of said plaintiff, before and under the direction of the undersigned, who was, by the said order, appointed referee, to conduct such personal surgical inspection and examination.

I do respectfully report that, pursuant to said order, the said Margaret Sarah Walsh, on the nineteenth day of November, A.D. 1868, did attend and appear before me at No. 100 East Twenty-second Street, the residence of the said William H. Van Buren, M.D., and did submit the affected part of her body to the inspection and examination of the said surgeons and the defendant, and an inspection and examination of the affected part of her body was then and there made by the said surgeons and by the defendant, in my presence and in the presence of the said John F. Walsh, her guardian, and of Mary Bowers, her aunt, who was present at the desire of said John F. Walsh, and, also, in the presence of Ira Shafer, Esq., and P. J. Gage, Esq., counsel for the defendant.

All of which is very respectfully submitted.

JOHN J. TOWNSEND, Referee.

November 21, 1868.

[Copy.]

Report of surgical experts appointed by the Court:

NEW YORK, Nov. 19th, 1868.

By the order of Judge Jones, of the Superior Court, we have this day examined the person of Margaret Sarah Walsh, a girl between 7 and 8 years of age, who, through her father as guardian, has charged Dr. Lewis A. Sayre with having punctured her left hip-joint, letting out its synovial fluid, producing a disease of the same, and thereby disabling her for life.

The girl was in a tolerably good condition, walked well without limping, both feet being naturally on the floor without any distortion of the body.

We then removed her clothing, and laying her on a sofa on her back, . . the limbs could be extended to their full length, so that the thighs and calves of each leg touched the sofa without any tilting of the pelvis. The two limbs were then very carefully measured by each of us, and were found to be of exactly the same length, viz. : $20\frac{3}{4}$ inches.

The right limb could be flexed so as to bring the knee to the chin ; the left one could not be flexed so freely, but could be brought to an acute angle with the pelvis. Rotation, abduction, and adduction were free, and without any pain whatever concussion upon the knee, or over the trochanter major, gave no evidence of pain. Passing the fingers firmly into the illiac fossæ of both sides, no swelling could with firm pressure be detected, or pain produced. There was a small dimpled-like depression above and behind the trochanter major, on the gluteal muscles, which the father stated was the scar which followed Dr. Sayre's operation. Dr. Sayre also testified that this was the place where he punctured the abscess at the time he first saw the patient, and we are fully convinced from the position of the cicatrix and the condition of the hip-joint, that it was not punctured at the time of the operation performed by

Dr. Sayre, as charged in the complaint. There was no devia
tion, or tenderness of the entire spinal column. There was an
open ulcer on the outer and posterior portion of the thigh, about
4 inches below the hip-joint, and another near the sacro-illiac
junction, the edges of which were inflamed; and there was
considerable inflammation and infiltration in the cellular tissue
around them, which probably was the obstruction to the perfectly free flexion and adduction of the thigh on that side.

There was considerable pain on pressure, and fullness over
the sacro-illiac junction, and it is our opinion that this was the
normal seat of the disease, and that the coxo-femoral articula-
tion was in a perfectly normal condition, as it is at present.

(Signed)   WM. H. VAN BUREN, M.D.,
FRANK H. HAMILTON, M.D.,
ERNEST KRACKOWIZER, M. D.

[Copy.]

PHILADELPHIA, Nov. 19th, 1868,
S. E. Corner 11th and Walnut Sts.

Dear Doctor : Your letter of the 14th inst., which is, however
post-marked the 18th, reached me to-day.

On the 2nd of last April, I spent a portion of the morning at
your office, and remember distinctly every thing that occurred
whilst I was there. Towards half-past eleven o'clock a woman
brought in a little girl, whom I imagined was about seven
years old. You had your assistant strip her, and you
remarked to Dr. Neftel, myself, and others, that these patients
should be invariably nude. There was not the slightest evidence of hip-disease. You ran your hand down the child's
spine and found that there was no deviation. You dwelt upon the
fact that "the gluteo-femoral crease of each side was at a right
angle with the rama-nates, thereby proving that the hip was
not affected. The child was placed prone upon your sofa or
lounge. A swelling was detected in the left gluteal region,

about the diagnosis of which there was some doubt. It was said, on the one hand, to be fatty tumor. There was an obscure sense of fluctuation, and I pronounced it a cyst of some kind, probably a chronic abscess. To clear up the diagnosis, you introduced a small exploring instrument. The point moved freely in a cavity, but nothing more than a little blood at first passed from the canula. On moving the latter, however, about and making pressure, pus made its appearance. You then punctured the abscess with your bistoury, making an incision about eight lines long, the pus spurted out in a full stream upon your office floor. Into the opening thus made you afterwards poured some carbolic oil.

The child made a good deal of noise, and the mother seemed to be dissatisfied during the whole procedure. Having washed our hands, Neftel and I joined you at lunch, after which I drove with you in the coupe.

I remember the entire occurrence perfectly, and will be glad to place myself at your disposal if you desire it. Should you wish me to come over, command me.

You certainly did not puncture the hip-joint, and you remarked this—" That pus may be connected with dead bone, *and it may be a mile off*. It may be from way up there,"—placing your finger on the middle dorsal spines. The idea of disease of the joint did not enter into any of our heads.

Truly your friend,

SAM. W. GROSS, M.D.

Prof. LEWIS A. SAYRE, M.D.

[Copy.]

126 W. 42D STREET, October 11th, 1868.

DR. SAYRE, *Dear Sir*:—In answer to your question I will state that soon after my arrival from Europe, I recollect having seen in your office, a girl suffering, as was thought, from a tumor on her back. She was accompanied by her mother. You examined her in my presence, found fluctuation, and concluded that the pretended tumor was nothing but an accumulation of pus, originating, as you thought, either from diseased vertebra, or hip-joint. You then introduced an exploring needle near the gluteal muscles, and, as was expected, pus came out.

I positively recollect that the needle did not touch a bone or any joint.

I will attend at the Superior Court Chambers at 11 o'clock, and will confirm these statements.

Your obedient servant,
W. NEFTEL.

New York, July 27th, 1868.

Sometime in April, 1868, Mrs. Walsh brought a child about six years old, to Dr. Sayre's office. I was at that time his assistant, and examined the child in the lower office, and found a round, tolerably firm swelling in the left gluteal region, which had the appearance and feeling of a tumor. I then carried the child into Dr. Sayre's private office for his examination, and he pronounced it an abscess. Some other medical gentlemen were present, and examined it at that time. Dr. Sayre then requested me to get an exploring needle, which he passed into the tumor. After withdrawing the needle pus escaped through the canula. He then withdrew it, and with a bistoury enlarged the opening about half an inch, cutting through the skin and superficial fascea. Pus gushed out in a stream; I should think from four to five ounces escaped. The mother then became excited, and, seizing the child, said she did not wish to have an operation performed, had rather it would die, &c., &c. She ran out of the office with it in her arms. It was with great difficulty that I could properly dress the abscess, as the mother continually ran around the office with the child. The opening was in the most prominent part of the abscess, near the crest of the illium, the abscess forming in front of the gluteal muscles.

Dr. Sayre did not open the hip-joint, nor go within two inches of it.

O. S. PAINE, M.D.,

9 East 31st Street.

———————

The cause, after having been reached on the regular call of the calendar of causes by the Court, at June Term, 1869, it remained ready for trial for nearly a year. The plaintiff's counsel failing to move the case for trial, it was thereupon by defendant's counsel brought to trial the 18th day of May, 1870, before the Court (Justice Jones presiding), and a jury then im-pannelled, when Mr. James offered to defendant's counsel to re-fer the cause to referees for trial, which offer was at once declined by the defendant and his counsel, they preferring to go to trial before a jury. The case thereupon proceeded to trial, Mr. James in his opening address stating he would prove the damages to the plaintiff, by the testimony of two of the most distinguished surgeons in America, if not in the world—Drs. Willard Parker and J. Murray Carnochan—and thereupon called them as witnesses, when they failing to appear, Mr. James stated that it was impossible for him to proceed with the trial without these, his most important witnesses, and asked for an attachment to compel their attendance, which was granted by the Court. The issue and return of such attachment, and the production of these witnesses before the Court thereunder, necessarily, occupying so much time as to endanger the trial of the cause going over for the term, the defendant and his coun-sel at the urgent solicitation of plaintiff's counsel, consented that the cause be sent to referees for trial, whereupon the following order was made and entered by the Court:

At a Special Term of the Superior Court of the City of
New York, on the 18th day of May, 1870.

Present: Hon. Samuel Jones, Justice.

Margaret Sarah Walsh, an infant, by
John F. Walsh, her guardian,

against

Lewis A. Sayre.

On the pleadings and proceedings in this action, and on the
consent of the attorneys of the respective parties hereto, and of
the parties thereto in open Court, it is ordered that this cause
be, and the same is hereby referred to John Swinburne, M.D.,
Wm. C. Traphagen and Thomas M. North, to hear and determine all the issues in the same, and each of them.

(A copy).   JAMES M. SWEENY, Clerk.

At a Special Term of the Superior Court of the City of New York, held at the Court House. in the City of New York, on the 28th day of May, 1870.

Present: Hon. SAMUEL JONES, Justice.

MARGARET SARAH WALSH, an infant, by JOHN F. WALSH, her guardian,

against

LEWIS A. SAYRE.

Upon reading and filing the foregoing annexed consent of the attorneys of the respective parties, and of the parties hereto, and on motion of P. J. Gage, of counsel for the defendant, it is hereby ordered that Benjamin Estes, Esq., Attorney and Counselor at Law, be, and he is hereby substituted as referee herein, to hear and determine all the issues herein joined, in the place and stead of Thomas M. North, Esq., appointed as one of the referees herein, by order made and entered herein, on the 18th day of May, 1870, Hon. Samuel Jones, Justice, presiding, that such order, dated May 18th, 1870, be and the same is hereby so modified, and that this order be entered *nunc pro tunc* as of the 18th day of May, 1870.

(A copy). JAMES M. SWEENY, Clerk.

SUPERIOR COURT.

MARGARET SARAH WALSH, an infant, by
JOHN F. WALSH, her guardian,

against

LEWIS A. SAYRE.

— — — — — — — —

Before W. C. TRAPHAGEN, Esq., Dr. SWINBURNE, and BENJA-
MIN ESTES, Esq., Referees.

May 28, 1870.

The referees primarily appointed were W. C. Traphagen,
Esq., Dr. Swinburne, and Thos. M. North, Esq., and at 10 A.
M., on the 28th of May, 1870, they and the parties and counsel
appeared at the office of Mr. Traphagen. For the plaintiff
were Messrs. James and Croak, and for the defendant Messrs.
McKean and Gage. The two referees first named took their
seats, but Mr. North, upon being requested to act, said : " I
came here to say that I could not join you as acting referee in
the case ; I cannot serve as referee."

Mr. JAMES : I wish I had known that before.

Mr. NORTH : I said so at once when appointed.

Mr. GAGE : Would Mr. North have any objections to state his
reasons for not serving ?

Mr. NORTH : Simply because I am not impartial between the
parties.

Mr. JAMES : Are you acquainted with Dr. Sayre ?

Mr. NORTH : I have known him for a number of years.

Dr. SAYRE : I happened to be talking to Mr. North when Mr.
Shafer came along. I did not know anything about its being

referred, but I thought it would be referred to three doctors. They laughed at the idea, and Mr. Shafer mentioned Mr. North's name because, I suppose, he saw me talking with Mr. North; but the latter said he could not serve, because he was a personal friend of mine.

Mr. North: The peculiarity of my position, which Mr. Shafer did not know, was that I have myself been a patient of the doctor and had members of my family under his care, and so I should start with a prepossession for his skill which would disqualify me from acting.

Mr. Traphagen: I was going to suggest that we might go on and take the testimony, and it would be decided—

Mr. James: I would like to make my statement before we go on; I would suggest that Mr. Traphagen name another referee.

Mr. Traphagen: I would rather that you settle it among yourselves; I would not like to assume any such responsibility.

Mr. North here suggested that perhaps his partner, Mr. Sedgwick, would act, and proceeded to the office to ascertain; but in a short time an answer came that Mr. Sedgwick's services could not be obtained.

Mr. Croak then suggested the name of Mr. Estes, of the firm of Brower & Estes, 229 Broadway. The counsel for defendant expressed their willingness to have that gentleman, when Mr. Croak proceeded to Mr. Estes' office and returned with him.

Mr. Traphagen then said; I see there are two suits; do you propose to try them together?

Mr. James: I suppose both should be tried and the evidence of one will decide the other.

Mr. Gage: I should not, in the absence of Mr. Shafer, who is associated with us, like to consent to that, but no doubt that may be arranged hereafter; I would not, however, like to enter our consent to that to-day. We will go on with the first case, that of Margaret Sarah Walsh, an infant, by John F. Walsh, her guardian, against Lewis A. Sayre.

Mr. JAMES : How is the report to be made ; is it understood that two have power to make a report ?

Mr. TRAPHAGEN : I should suppose so, that two might make the report, and the other might also make a report if he wishes.

Mr. JAMES : There is another matter which I wish to have settled, and that is as to the expense of these meetings ; I want that distinctly understood.

Mr. TRAPHAGEN : The feeling of the referees is that the counsel on both sides should make some arrangement as to what should be the compensation, and also whether the sessions continue the whole day or from hour to hour.

Mr. JAMES : I would now state to you shortly the nature of the case that has been referred to the tribunal that I have now the honor of addressing. It is a matter of very serious conse-quence to Mr. Walsh, the plaintiff, who is a gentleman in moderate circumstances, and I need not state that the issue of this is of great consequence to Dr. Sayre, professionally and otherwise. I agreed to this tribunal very readily, because this is an issue which requires the application of considerable intel-ligence, and I thought the matter would be better inquired into by it than by the ordinary materials of a jury. The substance of the complaint is want of skill—commonly called malpractice —in the defendant in his duty as a surgeon in the performance of an operation on a little girl, the daughter of Mr. and Mrs. Walsh, to whom they are devotedly attached, on the 18th of March, 1868.

Now, I am perfectly aware that, in these cases there may be said to be some difficulty on the part of the plaintiff. Dr. Sayre is a gentleman, I believe, of old eminence in his profession; but Dr. Sayre will allow me to say that I have known instances and shall cite instances where gentlemen quite as eminent as he have been held responsible for want of skill. Haste, incaution, perhaps sometimes a want of care in dealing with patients who are not so rich as others; I do not impute improper motives, but I have had some experience in hospitals and other places, and it is frequently the case. You will remember the case of the action against Sir Astley Cooper, who will be admitted by every medical man to be the first surgeon of the age. He was, however, held responsible in an action for an operation. Therefore, surgeons of great eminence and skill are as likely to fall into mistakes and malpractice, and show want of skill in matters done in a hurry, as he. On the 18th of March, this little child, who was about six years of age, had a swelling in her hip-joint. She had been attended by a medical man who will be called before you, an unpretending man, but a man of some skill as an apothecary and surgeon; but Mrs. Walsh was directed by the plaintiff to take her daughter to Dr. Sayre, not for an operation but for his opinion on the case. Now in addressing gentlemen of your experience in these matters, I need hardly call your attention to the great difference which has always been held, not only socially but in point of law, between an error of judgment on the part of a physician and skill on the part of a surgeon. A physician who prescribes treatment for certain symptoms proposed to him, where it is a mere question of judgment as to skill and experience, has a larger range and larger limit in the opinions which may arise from a want of judgment, than in the case of a manual operation. In this case of manual operation, when a person professes to be a surgeon and professes to operate skillfully, negligence is more easily fixed than in the case of a physician who goes through the diagnosis of a disease. The greatest man may err in fathoming the great secrets of nature. There is a total difference between want of skill and the undertaking of a manual operation. I will merely mention this that a broad distinction is taken by courts of law and natural justice between the judgment of a physician and the want of skill on the part of an operator.

Upon the 18th of March, 1868, this little girl, then six years of age, was taken to Dr. Sayre. The mother being the first witness whom I shall put upon the stand; she will describe what occurred. She saw Dr. Sayre in the act of taking some probe or surgical instrument and she objected to any operation —the objection of the child amounts to nothing—but she objected strongly against any operation being performed. She desired the child not to be operated upon, but wished to have further advice. I mention this, not charging the doctor with any want of humanity, but say that there was a haste and recklessness and want of care in the course of this operation. He operated on the poor child, and what we charge is that, in probing the wound, Dr. Sayre so unskillfully managed it that—

Mr. Gage: Perhaps you had better take the pleadings?

Mr. James: I think I am stating the matter correctly. We charge in substance that he so unskillfully managed the operation that the synovial fluid was allowed to escape. The portion of the system which encloses that fluid (which the learned referees know, is that fluid which is created for the purpose of lubricating the joints, and when wanting, the joints become stiff) was punctured in some way or other, and the synovial fluid escaped. That is the substance of the charge.

Now there cannot be—I defy all the medical men whom he can call—if this is true; there cannot be any question as to want of skill, no more than if an uneducated man thrust a probe through an artery, or through the jugular vein, or where he was bound to know that an artery existed. If it is true that by this puncture of the wound, that by this operation so made, the synovial fluid was brought from that joint, it has been the cause of everlasting injury to the unhappy child. It has been a permanent injury, and, as one celebrated surgeon, who will be called before you in this case said, the child will either die as the result of the operation, or be injured for life. Therefore, if it be true that this synovial fluid, in the course of the operation,

was punctured, or the parts containing it were so injured—if
that fact be true, I do not care if all the physicians and surgeons that ever existed were brought, there is not a gentleman
who dare go on the stand and say that the puncture in the hip
of a human being, which is so unskillfully done (and it must be
unskillfully done), as to allow the fluid to escape, that that is not
negligence on the part of the surgeon. I rely upon it then that
if that be true, if the highest men in the profession in the city
saw the fluid escaping from the operation for weeks afterwards—
if I establish that fact, I will show you by treatises, by evidence,
and by evidence of two of the first physicians in the city, that
there was negligence. When instructions are given to an attorney to attend to a case, and he never went near the Court, the
act of omission would be evidence of negligence which nothing
could remove. The poor child has been, since the operation,
in the most serious condition. We had a great struggle
for the production of the child before the suit, but such
production was objected to on principle. There will be nothing concealed from the referee ; you will have a history
of the child from the moment she left Dr. Sayre, to the
moment she is produced before you. The answer put on the
record is this, that if there were any negligence (I am speaking
substantially as regards it), if there were any negligence, it was
the negligence of the father and mother. Why, these poor people have done nothing except to employ physicians and surgeons, and therefore any such notion is perfectly ridiculous. I
believe the defendant relies on the fact that he said to them to
bring him the child again, but they took further advice, which
will be given in evidence. You will hear evidence of what the
treatment of the child has been. The father has toiled hard to
get her to some state of health, which the evidence will show
she never can attain to. That is the state of the case. This
child is permanently injured for life, and it is a matter upon
which I should insult you, if I say anything about the question
of damages.

Dr. Swinburne : You merely charge that she took the child

to Dr. Sayre for an operation, without stating if there was any disease in the child?

Mr. James: We took the child to be looked at to try to ascertain the cause of the disease.

Dr. Swinburne: Do you claim the child was healthy when you took her to the doctor?

Mr. James: She was suffering from some disease in the hip. She would not have taken a healthy child.

Laura Agnes Walsh was then called by Mr. James, who being duly sworn, was examined by him as follows:

Q. Where do you reside?

A. 121 Charlton Street.

Q. Mr. Walsh, the plaintiff, is your husband?

A. Yes, sir.

Q. What is the name of your daughter Margaret?

A. Margaret Sarah Walsh.

Q. How old is she now?

A. She is eight years the 10th of February.

Q. Now in her ninth year?

A. Yes, sir.

Q. Well now, early in 1868 did you find that your daughter was suffering from something? Proceed and describe as near as you can what it was.

A. Her feet used to swell, and she could not walk very well. She would be sick and troublesome. I brought Dr. Vaughan to my house, but he said it was rheumatism. I thought that he might be mistaken, and the father told me to take her to Dr. Sayre.

Q. And it was at the suggestion of your husband that you took her to Dr. Sayre?

A. Yes, sir.

Q. Do you remember the day when you took her to Dr. Sayre?

A I could not exactly remember the day or month. I remember it was in 1868.

Mr. GAGE : She don't remember the day or month ?

WITNESS : No, the month of March, 1868.

By Mr. JAMES :

Q. You are quite sure it was in March, 1868 ?

A. Yes, sir, but I cannot say the date.

Q. About what time of the day did you take her ?

A. It was about noon—no, from 12 to 1.

Q. Did you see Dr. Sayre ?

A. Yes, sir.

Q. Tell the learned gentlemen exactly what passed and what you said to him in the first instance ?

A. I told him that the child was ill, and for some time the child was getting delicate in her system and did not use to walk right with one foot, and I told him just like that. I wished him, I said, to examine it, but I did not want any operation.

Q. You did not say anything about an operation then : then you said you wanted him to examine her ; where was this ?

A. It was in his house.

Q. What was done ?

A. He told me to undress her, and I did so, and he turned around and said the child had no spine disease or hip disease He then called to one to bring him something, and what he brought him he ran through the hip. He never told me what he was going to do. I then went to dress the child. He said he was not done with the child. I said. do not do anything more to-day ; if necessary, I will bring her again, but he got some doctors to hold her, and kept cutting her. I tried to get out of the room, but the child roared and I had to go back to the child.

Q. After the child was undressed, you heard him tell some gentleman to bring some instrument ; did you see it ?

A. No, I did not see it or hear what was said, I only heard him say to bring something to him.

Q. What did you say about not operating ; did you mention it then ?

A. He had the thing through her before I knew what he was going to do; I did not want him to do anything more; I said, if necessary, I would bring her again.

Q. Did you see where the instrument went?

A. It went through the hip, the hole is there yet, and a dozen more yet.

By Mr. GAGE : From the same operation?

By Mr. JAMES :

Q. After you saw it go through the hip was any other operation made?

A. It seemed to be with knives he cut her. The first thing seemed to be small, but the other instruments seemed to be more like knives.

Q. Did you see them?

A. I could give no opinion about them.

Q. Did you see the flesh?

A. I saw the body.

Q. Did you see the child being operated upon?

A. I saw the blood and water come out; I saw that plain.

Judge McKEAN : We do not mean to be technical, but we wish that the learned counsel would not put leading questions. We should prefer him to examine her in the ordinary way.

Mr. JAMES : Which is the question that is leading or suggesting?

Judge McKEAN : I must say you have asked a few that were.

Mr. JAMES : State what it is and I will withdraw it.

(Continuing).

Q. Now state what happened?

A. He bandaged her up and told me to take her home, and somebody would see her the next day.

Q. Did he tell you the name of any person?

A. He did not mention any name, but I remember him saying, "Dr. Paine, you will go and see the child to-morrow."

Mr. GAGE: State what you know and not what you think.

WITNESS: I would not be sure that it was Dr. Paine.

By Mr. JAMES:

Q. State to the best of your recollection if he mentioned any name, and what it was?

A. To the best of my recollection he mentioned Dr. Paine's name.

Q. Did you take the child home?

A. I took her home, and I waited for a time that the doctor would come.

Q. What time did you get home?

A. About 2 o'clock, or a little after.

Q. Did any one call from Dr. Sayre to your house?

A. Never until after the suit was commenced, and then Dr. Sayre came once.

Q. At this time was any medical man in attendance upon your child?

A. Dr. Vaughan.

Q. Did Dr. Vaughan see the child after the operation, and if so, how soon?

A. The same evening.

Q. Did he examine it with the bandage taken off?

A. Yes, sir.

Q. Were the bandages taken off?

A. Yes, sir, the bandages were taken off.

Q. What was the state of the child at that time?

Mr. GAGE: That is objected to; the witness has not been shown to be an expert, and the question must imply the answer of an expert.

Mr. TRAPHAGEN: We propose to allow the question, although we think probably it would be better to lay some foundation. but we will take it for what it is worth.

Mr. GAGE: You will please note the objection.

(Witness answering): She went on very low; after the

operation it lay down and could not put her feet under her, and now the wound or matter run out all the time; it would run in streams; you would think it would never stop; then her father and Dr. Vaughan took her to Dr. Parker, and then they know.

Q. Did you see stuff exuding or running from the wound?

A. There was something between whiteish and yellowish stuff; it is running yet; it can be seen.

Q. Did Dr. Vaughan see the child on the following day?

A. He saw her that evening.

Q. Did he see her the following day?

A. I can't remember.

Q. What was done : was the child taken to Dr. Parker?

Mr. GAGE: We object to a leading question.

Mr. TRAPHAGEN: It is immaterial as to that fact.

By Mr. JAMES:

Q. Was the child taken to Dr. Parker?

A. That night after she went to sleep, she raged and screamed about the Dr. Sayre and butter knives so, that I never would take her again.

Q. Then was she taken to him?

A. Yes, sir.

Q. When?

A. About the beginning of June.

Q. Was she taken to Dr. Carnochan?

A. He was brought to the house.

Q. Which saw her first?

A. Dr. Parker saw her first.

Q. Fix the time as near as you can when the child was taken to Dr. Parker?

A. I think it was about the 5th of June.

Q. Who took the child to Dr. Parker?

A. Her father and Dr. Vaughan.

Q. Was the child afterwards seen by Dr. Carnochan?

A. Yes, two weeks after that.

Q. Where did Dr. Carnochan see the child?

A. In my own house.

Q. In June, at the time your husband took the little girl to the Doctor (Parker), was Dr. Vaughan in attendance upon her?

A. Yes, sir, he was still in attendance.

Q. How long did Dr. Vaughan attend the child from March, 1868?

A. He attended her all the time until he got sick.

Q. How long ago was that?

A. It is about a year ago.

Q. What is the state of the child now as to its hip?

A. The hip is running.

Q. Running now?

A. Yes, sir, and she is all crooked to one side, and as for her life, it is living and suffering she is; at night she is crying with pain; no strength at all, and the little limbs are soft and hanging down.

Q. Has that sore or wound been running ever since the operation?

A. It has, ever since; never stopped.

Q. Is it the same sore now, or did it heal up?

A. That healed up, but there are other sores.

Mr. GAGE: We object to that.

By Mr. JAMES:

Q. How near to the spot which was operated upon did the sore break out?

A. There are several sores; one healed up.

Q. How near?

A. They all go round about.

Q. Can you tell us, of your own knowledge, about how soon the part that was operated upon—the wound from the operation—closed?

A. It was about five months.

Q. Was that open for five months?

A. Yes; open for five months.

Q. Was that wound open when Dr. Parker and Dr. Carnochan saw the child ?

· A. Yes, sir.

Q. Do I understand you that the wound closed in about five months ?

A. Yes.

Q. How soon after did sores appear ?

A. Before this closed there was another gathering, and it broke right away after this one closed.

Q. You say before ?

A. There was another one at the time this closed, and broke at the time.

Cross-examined by Judge McKean :

Q. I suppose you went to Mr. James and made your statement of the case before this suit was brought ?

A. No, sir ; this is the first statement I have given.

Q. Did you not converse with Mr. James about it ?

A. No, sir.

Q. From whom then, if you know, did Mr. James get the information ?

Mr. JAMES : I will tell you; from Mr. Walsh and Mr. Vaughan.

By Judge McKEAN :

Q. You never informed him ?

A. No, sir.

Q. Did you know, Mrs. Walsh, what the complaint was, as prepared by Mr. James, in this case ?

A. I knew the complaint in the suit, and what was alleged, to be true.

Q. Did you know what the complaint was, that is, the terms of the complaint; did you hear it read ?

A. Oh yes, sir.

Q. About the time the suit was brought ?

A. Yes, sir.

Q. Mrs. Walsh, you remarked that the little girl had been ailing before you took her to Dr. Sayre; about how long?

A. She was a year ailing before that; the May before the March she was operated upon Dr. Vaughan took her to Dr. Sayre to make an examination.

Q. Nearly a year?

A. Nearly a year, and he said there was nothing the matter with the child he could find out.

Q. Were you present?

A. No, sir.

Q. When the little girl was taken you were not present?

A. No, sir.

Q. Mrs. Walsh, you had frequently seen the person of the little girl before you took her to him?

A. Yes, sir.

Q. Was there not upon her person, near the left hip—I believe it was the left hip?

A. Yes, sir, the left hip.

Q. Was there not a swelling there when you took her to Dr. Sayre?

A. I could not say there was a swelling, and her flesh was of the same color; no redness or no inflammation, or no appearance that any one could see; she was as perfect in her appearance as any person was; if there were a swelling it could not be discerned.

Q. Well, you noticed a swelling?

A. No, I cannot state that I did.

Q. State again what you said to the Doctor; what you asked him to do when you took her there?

A. I told him how she had been there before, and how she could walk, and at other times she could not walk so well; I wanted him to examine her, and if there was anything wrong to tell me.

Q. Whom did you see first?

A. I went in the basement first, and there were some strange men there; some might be patients and others might be Doctors.

Q. Was she not examined in the basement first by Dr. Paine, or somebody?

A. No one at all; I spoke to no one except Dr. Sayre.

Q. Well, Mrs. Walsh, I want to read a sentence from the complaint and then to ask you a question : " Third. That Mar-" garet Sarah Walsh, the infant daughter of this plaintiff, on or " about the 10th day of March, was taken to defendant to be " treated by him for an injury in the neighborhood of one of her " hips, and the cause of which injury was unknown to the " mother ;" was that true ?

A. Well, I thought there might be something in her hip.

Q. And you took her for the purpose, as stated in the complaint ?

A. I asked him to examine her ; I was afraid there might be something the matter with the hip.

Q. I read the sentence from the complaint in which it is stated that you took the child to Dr. Sayre, he being a surgeon as aforesaid, to be treated by him for a swelling or injury in the neighborhood of one of the hips, etc. ; that is a fact, is it not?

A. The swelling was very slight.

Q. No ; but you took her there to be treated by Dr. Sayre ?

A. I took her for an examination, and get him, if he could, to tell me what was the matter with her.

Q. You have said that already several times, but you do not answer the question ; did you not take her to be treated for a swelling or something ?

A. I took her there to be treated to explain what was the matter ; he said she had no hip disease or spine disease.

Q. He then made an explanation and then proceeded with the treatment ?

A. He did not proceed at all, he said he would send a man, but did not.

Judge McKean : I hope the referee will not take down anything irresponsive.

Q. You did not see, then, the whole operation, as you say ?

A. I saw him put the instrument through her, but I turned my head aside and could not see him cut my child up like a—

Q. Now after he put the instrument in, did anything come out of her person where he put it in ?

A. There was something which appeared like water and something like a hard substance, I thought, came with it, something that looked like flesh—some kind of a substance.

Q. Did not one gentleman take a basin and catch the discharge ?

A. I did not see it.

Q. You were considerably excited ?

A. It is very likely that I was.

Q. Mrs. Walsh, did you see whether there was any discharge after he put the first instrument in ?

A. No discharge like matter ; there was something like water that came out the first time.

Q. Did it come out through a tube ?

A. I could not tell ; I could not tell what it looked like.

Q. You do not know whether the first time he used a cutting instrument or piercing instrument ?

A. It was a piercing instrument, something sharp and small.

Q. Can you tell whether the discharge came out through an open wound or tube ?

A. It came out of the wound.

Q. Was there a tube in the wound ?

A. No ; he took it right out again and this ran down the hip.

Q. After he used the first instrument did he use another instrument ?

A. He walked away and spoke to those with him, and I went to dress the child, but he said, " I am not done with the child." The child was near dead and I was, too ; I said, " do not do anything more, I will bring her some other day ;" he then took the child and the doctors held her, and he commenced to cut her ; I closed my eyes, but once I opened my eyes and saw blood and water run out.

Q. You did not see all that occurred ?

A. I could not look.

Q. Did you hear, and can you relate what was said?

A. I cannot remember anything where he spoke to those, only one time he said the child had no hip disease or spine disease.

Q. Then he gave an opinion?

A. Yes, before he cut her.

Q. You proceeded to dress the child when he said that he had not got done with her yet?

A. Yes.

Q. Did you keep on and dress her?

A. No, he would not let me; he took the child and—

Q. Then he performed the operation of cutting?

A. Yes.

Q. Then the child screamed?

A. She screamed when cutting her and after he put the instrument in.

Q. After the discharge of the second operation what did he do?

A. He bandaged her up then.

Q. Did he put any application on her?

A. He poured something out of a bottle.

Q. Did he not ask you to bring the child to him at a certain time?

A. Yes; he said bring her in two or three days again; but then he said there would be a doctor come the next day.

Q. What did you say to that when he asked you to bring the child in two or three days?

A. At the time I said I would.

Q. You were, of course, very much excited?

A. I was, of course; I was frightened, I am sure.

Q. Well, you did not take back the child again?

A. No, sir; I never did; when I came home and told Dr. Vaughan how the operation was performed, he said it was a wonder the child did not die under it.

Q. Never mind that; it was the first of June when you took the child, or when it was taken to Dr. Parker?

A. About the 5th of June.

Q. Did you go with her?

A. No, sir.

Q. Did the little girl walk about the house at that time?

A. Well, no; she might be able to put her foot under her; she could not walk alone; she had to be carried to the cars.

Q. And a considerable time after that she went—

A. Dr. Carnochan came to the house?

Q. At the time she was taken to Dr. Parker, were there any other openings or sores?

A. Not at that time.

Q. Now describe the location of these other sores; are they above or below, or in front of, or behind the other?

A. The first one came a little more down to the leg, a little under, well, it was not right up—I do not know how I could explain it; it was more down to the leg, and when the next sore came it was back.

Q. Let me ask you, was there a swelling before it broke out?

A. It inflamed up and broke open, and then it commenced running like the one that closed; the one that gathered commenced to run as the one that closed, the same kind of stuff.

Q. Where did the next one appear?

A. The next one came more back, on the back part, the fleshy part more.

Q. Did that appear like the other?

A. Yes, the same way; it inflamed and burst.

Q. Discharged corrupt matter?

A. Well, what you saw.

By Mr. Traphagen:

Q. The third one was on the fleshy part?

A. The fleshy part of the limb, the hip—the seat behind.

By Judge McKean:

Q. I think the swelling he operated upon was near the left hip?

A. On the left hip

Q. If I understand you, the sores are discharging now?

A. Yes, sir; between what is healed and what is running there are eight sores.

By Mr. ESTES:

Q. Eight discharging now?

A. No; between what is healed and running.

By Judge McKEAN:

Q. What are discharging now?

A. There are three discharging now.

Q. How many at once?

A. I thing there has been five at a time.

Q. About how much of this matter or corruption was discharged there in the office at Dr. Sayre's?

A. I don't remember any corruption of that kind at Dr. Sayre's.

Q. Well, whatever it was?

A. I could not tell; but there was a narrow stream ran down the side.

Q. After he cut it?

A. I shut my eyes and when I opened my eyes I saw it run.

Q. Do you remember any conversation among the physicians when you were present in regard to the nature of the difficulty?

A. I didn't hear a word; they didn't let me hear.

Q. They did not talk in whispers?

A. I do not remember a word that was said, only he told another Doctor that she had neither hip nor spine disease; they talked to themselves as talking about other things.

Q. Was anything said as to whether it was a tumor or abscess?

A. There was something about an abscess.

Q. Did you think anything was said as to whether it was a tumor or abscess?

A. I think it was an abscess.

Q. Do you know how many Doctors there were present?

A. As near as I can remember, there were four or six, I cannot say positively.

Q. Do you remember the names of any of them?

A. I remember Dr. Paine's name, that is all I remember.

Q. They stood by when the Doctor performed the operation?

A. Some of them held the child.

Q. Do you remember, Mrs. Walsh, when Dr. Sayre spoke of its being an abscess, what any other of the physicians said?

A. I do not remember what reply they made.

Q. You do not remember whether they said it was a tumor or—

A. I don't remember what they said.

Q. I think. Mrs. Walsh, you had the little girl in Court on Thursday when the case was referred ; I think she was walking with you on the street?

A. Oh, yes, she can walk now.

Q. Though feeble, she walks pretty well?

A. If she walks two blocks she says she is tired.

Q. Then she complains of weakness?

A. She is not as large now as a year before she was operated upon.

Q. After walking, or playing about, or standing for a while, of what does she complain?

A. She complains of a soreness in the hip and of being tired. and she is weak ; she has no appetite and is weak, although she has had the best of treatment that could be given.

By Mr. TRAPHAGEN :

Q. The evening the bandage was removed, the first evening after the operation was performed by Dr. Sayre, was there any discharge?

A. I think there was something that ran out then.

Q. What had it the appearance of?

A. Something like milk, between a yellow and a milky color.

By Dr. Swinburne :

Q. You say that it has continued to run ever since ?
A. Yes, Sir.

By Mr. Traphagen :

Q. After you left him, you called in Dr. Vaughan ?
A. I came home first.
Q. Then you called in Dr. Vaughan and you removed the bandage, which, you or the Doctor ?
A. I do not remember.

By Judge McKean :

Q. Mrs. Walsh, describe the chunks that came out with the discharge ?
A. I could not describe them.
Q. About how large should you think they were ?
A. Well, just a little bit less than the end of the finger. It appeared like something hard ; it did not look like matter.
Q. Like putrid flesh ?
A. No, not like putrid flesh.
Q. It was not entirely fluid ?
A. There was a stream that ran like pure water, and there was one time that I thought I saw something in it, but I cannot say whether it was something of her hip, or whether it came out.
Q. What was the color ?
A. It was more whitish.
Q. Was this on the floor, or in the basin ?
A. I could not tell, I cannot explain what it was I saw there. I saw the clear water run out, that was the most I could discern.
Q. You spoke of the doctor's cutting, you do not mean to say he cut any portion of the flesh away ; he cut an opening in the abscess ?
A. I could not tell whether he cut the flesh away or not ; he might have cut plenty of flesh inside, for all I know.

Q. You do not know anything about that?

A. No.

By Dr. SWINBURNE:

Q. Did this piece float in the water or sink?

A. Whatever he put in, when he pulled it out, the water like ran, and I thought there was a little hard substance that ran after it.

Q. About as large as the end of the finger?

A. Something smaller than that.

By Judge McKEAN:

Q. Did it come through the tube?

A. After he took the tube out.

Mr. TRAPHAGEN: After the water was running.

By Dr. SWINBURNE:

Q. Did you examine it afterwards?

A. No, I did not see it at all; that is, one glimpse I got, so frightened me that I gave one look and ran away. There was only one sign of a piece, but I cannot tell whether it was on her hip, or came out with the water.

Mr. CROAK: I find that Mr. James, before he left, neglected to prove the guardianship of Mr. Walsh; will you admit that?

Mr. GAGE: Our pleadings put him on the proof; we have not seen any order.

Mr. TRAPHAGEN: You can prove that at the next meeting.

Mr. ESTES: You can prove that by documentary evidence.

Mr. GAGE: Yes.

(Adjourned to Thursday, 2d June, 1870, at 3 o'clock P.M.)

SUPERIOR COURT.

MARGARET SARAH WALSH, an infant, by
JOHN F. WALSH, her guardian,

against

LEWIS A. SAYRE.

June 2d, 1870.

Amariah B. Vaughan, sworn, examined by Mr. JAMES :

Q. What is your occupation, surgeon or physician ?
A. Physician.

Q. Where were you practising in 1868, at the time of this operation ?
A. In the 9th ward of New York City.

Q. What street and number ?
A. My residence at that time was 703 Greenwich Street ; that was where I generally stopped.

Q. Now, do you know Mr. Walsh, the father of this little girl, and the whole family ?
A. Yes, sir ; well.

Q. How long have you known them ?
A. I guess I have known them some 10 or 12 years altogether.

Q. Do you remember being called in to attend the little girl Margaret ?
A. Yes, sir.

Q. Can you tell us about the time you first attended her medically ?
A. Oh, well I attended the family, I can not tell positively, because I have attended the family ; have seen first one and then the other.

Q. How long have you attended the family ?
A. For that length of time.

Q. You know the little girl, do you not?

A. Yes, sir : since her birth.

Q. Do you remember the fact of her going to Dr. Sayre and undergoing this operation, and the fact of seeing her afterwards?

A. I saw her after I was informed she had been taken to Dr. Sayre, and the operation had been performed.

Q. To the best of your recollection, how shortly after the operation did you see the child?

A. Well, within the first 24 hours, I think, after they informed me the operation had been performed.

Q. Where was she when you saw her?

A. At her father's.

Q. Well, but in what position, sitting up or lying down?

A. She was lying down.

Q. In bed?

A. She was on the lounge at the time.

Q. As near as you can, just state, was the wound bandaged or open when you first saw it?

A. I did not examine the wound at the time—at that particular time. I prescribed for the child because the system was in a perfect state of nervous prostration.

Q. You found her in a perfect state of nervous prostration?

A. Yes, sir.

Q. When did you first have your attention directed to the wound itself ; how soon, to the best of your recollection?

A. It was at the first time ; the first or second visit I made there I examined it.

Q. How soon would that be after the operation?

A. I saw it within the first 24 or 48 hours.

Q. Did you examine the wound at that time after the operation?

A. I then removed the dressing.

Q. You are correct in stating that, within 24 or 48 hours, you removed the dressing?

A. I did not remove it particularly.

Q. Was it removed in your presence?

A. I have no recollection on that point.

Q. How soon did you see the wound after the operation ?

A. I say from 24 to 48 hours.

Q. Did you remove the dressing then, or was it removed by somebody else ?

A. I do not recollect.

Q. Was it removed by somebody so that you saw the wound ?

A. It amounted to really nothing, comparatively. The dressing was nothing but a simple bandage with the linen first, I believe, laid over. If I mistake not, the doctor that performed the operation had furnished liniment, or something to apply to it.

Q. That is not what I am asking ; how soon did you see the wound without the dressing ?

A. I have answered that.

Q. As near as you can recollect ?

By Mr. TRAPHAGEN :

Q. Within what time ?

A. Within the first 48 hours after.

By Mr. JAMES :

Q. Do you remember whether you removed it, or the mother ?

A. I do not recollect.

Q. Did you observe the wound ; did you examine it ; did you look at it and see it ?

A. I saw a discharge from the wound ; the wound was not very large.

Q. Did you see a discharge ?

A. Yes, sir.

Q. As a medical man, do you know what the synovial fluid is ?

A. I know its uses, of course.

Q. Do you its appearance ?

A. Yes, sir; I know its appearance.

Q. Just state now what the appearance is ?

A. It is perfectly colorless, transparent.

Q. Do you know, from its appearance, what it is when you see it?

A. Yes sir ; I have seen it a great many times.

Q. Now did you observe any synovial fluid :

(Objected to by Judge McKean).

By Mr. Traphagen : I suppose he had better tell what he did observe, if he knows.

By Mr. James :

Q. What did you observe ?

A. As far as I can judge in regard to the appearance—of course, we have to go into as far as it is possible to judge—I concluded it was synovial fluid.

Q. Did you see it ?

A. I saw it, and I supposed it to be it, from observation ; I made no microscopic examination of it.

Q. As far as your experience goes, can you detect it without a microscopic observation ?

A. Yes, sir ; it is very readily detected, for there is nothing that would secrete a fluid of that kind in such a position.

Q. It has a color, has it :

A. It is perfectly colorless ; it is a colorless fluid.

Q. What kind of substance does it present to the touch or sight ?

A. I would call it rather glutinous if you rub it down very slightly.

Q. Do you know the Greek derivation of the word ?

A. No, sir ; I do not.

Mr. James : Perhaps I can tell you. It is from the word ωον, an egg.

(Objected to by Mr. Gage.)

By Mr. JAMES :

Q. You say it is colorless ?

A. Yes, sir ; if it is—

Q. Do you know enough in your own experience and knowledge, as a medical man, to state whether that was synovial fluid ?

A. That was, in my judgment.

Q. Did you remember the fact of advising that the child be afterwards taken to Dr. Parker, or did Mr. Walsh. How was that ?

A. I do not recollect.

Q. Do you remember the fact of the child being taken to Dr. Parker afterwards ?

A. I do.

Q. Did you go with the child ?

A. I was there ; yes, sir.

Q. From the time of the operation until the child was taken to Dr. Parker, did you attend her ?

A. I did, sir.

Q. About how long was it after the operation that she was taken to Dr. Parker, as near as you can say ?

A. As near as I can recollect, between a month and 6 weeks, about that.

Q. During that time from the operation until she was taken to Dr. Parker, did you attend her medically ?

A. I did.

Q. How frequently did you attend her ?

A. Well, that I can not recollect ; I was at the house almost every day.

Q. Once a week, or month, or every day ?

A. Generally every day I was seeing some of the family; I did not go over particularly to see her.

By Mr. GAGE : He did not go over particularly to see her.

(Objected to by Mr. James.)

Mr. Traphagen : I suppose he might suggest—.

Mr. Gage : That it might come to the ears of the Referees.

Mr. James :

Q. Well, whether you went to see her or the family, how frequently did you see her in the weeks from the time of the operation until she went to Dr. Parker ?

A. That I could not tell. It was, well, 2 or 3 days after the operation. I think I saw the child every day. I was there specially for the occasion.

Q. Did you treat her medically ?

A. The condition in which she was in : I did not treat her for the wound.

Q. Did you treat her at all ?

A. I did certainly.

Q. How did you treat her ; what way ; what did you give her ?

A. I gave her tonics, alteratives, and anodynes.

Q. Did you do anything with the wound ?

A. There was nothing done by me to the wound. The preparation was furnished Mrs. Walsh, and applied to the wound at the time the operation was performed ; I had nothing to do with that, sir.

Q. Was the wound treated ; was it bandaged ?

A. I understood from Mrs. Walsh that the preparations—

Q. Never mind what you understood. Did you see the wound in the interval from the operation until she was taken to Dr. Parker ?

A. I did see it often.

Q. Now, in reference to this synovial fluid, I think you have stated that you saw that upon the first occasion ; is that so ?

A. What I supposed to be it.

Q. Was it the synovial fluid ?

(Objected to by Mr. Shafer).

By Mr. James :

Q. How long did that fluid, which you supposed to be the synovial fluid, how long did it discharge ?

A. It would be impossible for me to tell.

Q. Up to the time she was taken to Dr. Parker, did it last ?

A. It must have been so, because Dr. Parker said—

(Objected to. Ordered to be stricken out.)

Q. How long did you observe what you supposed to be the synovial fluid exude from the wound ?

A. It is impossible for me to determine that.

Mr. Shafer : We do not object to what Dr. Parker pronounces it to be. The stenographer can take that.

Mr. Traphagen : It has been ruled out.

Mr. Shafer : We waive the objection, so it is not so.

Mr. James : I would rather that Dr. Parker would give an opinion.

Mr. Shafer : It is our part to say whether we waive the objection or not.

Mr. Traphagen : Upon your objection we have it stricken out.

By Mr. James :

Q. Can you state to the Referees how long you have observed any discharge of what you stated to be, in your opinion, the synovial fluid ?

A. I could not tell that, sir. I do not know at what time or how long it continued ; I do not recollect.

Q. Do you remember the fact of going with the child to Dr. Parker ?

A. Yes, sir.

Q. How shortly before that, to the best of your recollection, had you seen any discharge of what you supposed to be the synovial fluid?

A. I do not recollect.

Q. Did you recommend the child to be taken to Dr. Parker, or how did it come about?

A. I think that I did. I am not positive in regard to it. I think that I did.

Q. Were you present when Dr. Parker examined the wound?

A. Yes, sir.

Q. Were you present when Dr. Carnochan came to the house and examined the child?

A. I do not know that I was there at the time.

Q. Any part of the time when Dr. Carnochan was in the act of examining the child?

A. Yes, sir.

Q. Did you recommend Dr. Carnochan to be consulted or not?

A. I do not recollect whether I did or not. I think it very probable I was consulted in regard to it.

Q. Can you state to the Referees how frequently, and for how long a time you observed what in your opinion was the synovial fluid, after the operation?

A. I have no recollection in regard to it. It could not be for a great while, because there could not be any remaining there.

Q. Did the child get better or worse before being taken to Dr. Parker?

A. The child continued to fail in health, and has since the operation.

Q. Did Dr. Parker prescribe any treatment for the child?

A. Yes, sir.

Q. Did the child continue under your care after Dr. Parker had examined it and seen it?

A. Dr. Parker and myself concluded on the remedies to give, at least I gave. Dr. Parker prescribed for the child, and I continued the prescription ordered by him.

Q. How soon after he saw the child did Dr. Carnochan see it ?

A. I cannot recollect.

Q. Fifty years, fifty hours, or fifty weeks ?

A. I cannot recollect.

Q. About how long ?

A. I have no recollection, sir. I recollect the circumstance, but not the time.

Q. Did you continue the treatment prescribed by Dr. Parker for the child ?

A. Yes, sir; because they both concluded on the same; there was no alteration made by the doctor.

Q. You say Dr. Carnochan saw the child after Dr. Parker; was the treatment prescribed by Dr. Carnochan very much the same as Dr. Parker prescribed ?

A. Yes, sir.

Q. Was that continued by you after Dr. Carnochan had seen the child ?

A. Yes, sir, it was.

Q. What was it, as near as you can tell ?

A. The syrup of the phosphates and the syrup of iodide of iron—the solution of iodide of iron.

Q. How long was that treatment continued under the supervision of Dr. Carnochan ?

A. I do not recollect; for a long time, for months, with good diet, and recommendation from Dr. Carnochan to take her to the sea shore.

Q. You know that the child of your own knowledge had good diet supplied to it ?

A. I do.

Q. And you know the child was taken to the sea shore ?

A. I do not know, because I was not there. I do not know that she was.

Q. When were you last in attendance upon the child ?

A. I have seen the child, but not been in attendance for some time.

Q. When did your medical attendance on the child cease?

A. It has been more than a year since I was there.

Q. More than a year ago?

A. Yes, sir.

Q. Up to the time you were attending and applying this treatment to the child, did it get better or worse?

A. Well, in what way do you mean.

Q. I mean in health?

A. Her health remained nearly about the same.

Q. About the same?

A. Well, she was in better health before the operation than afterwards.

Q. Well, in reference to the hip joint, and the power of motion, how did that get on?

A. She has no power to amount to anything, so that you can see when she moves; you can notice it, which you could not before.

Q. When did you see the child last; what was the last time you saw her?

A. I saw her a few weeks ago, but not professionally, but simply as a visit; I made no examination at all; I simply saw the child.

Q. Is there any permanent injury there?

A. I suppose there is.

Q. In your judgment?

A. Yes, sir, that is so.

Q. In your judgment?

A. Yes, sir.

Q. How is the hip joint affected; what way?

A. That I have not examined; I could not tell positively.

Q. When did you examine it?

A. As I told you, she suffered a great deal of pain; there was a thickening of the periosteum—outside covering of the bone.

Q. Do you know whether that would result from a discharge of the synovial fluid?

A. It would not necessarily ; I do not see why it should.

Q. Is it one of the results of it ?

A. No, sir ; it was down below where the operation was performed : I mean the upper third of the thigh bone ; it was from the middle of the upper third to the centre of the middle third, the thickening of the periosteum.

Q. Will you describe on yourself where abouts this operation was performed, what part of the hip ?

A. The point where the thigh bone comes into the socket. The thickening was down here (placing his finger). The thigh bone is divided into three parts—the lower, the middle and upper third. This thickening took place there (again placing his finger), half way between the upper and middle third—equal distance probably.

Q. Where was the power of motion affected—the joint below, or, where you saw the child had not the same power of motion ; where was it affected—the muscular power of motion ?

A. The muscles were affected from want of use.

Q. How long did the wound after the operation remain open ?

A. I don't know, sir : but for a long time.

Q. About how long ?

A I can't determine positively.

Q. About ?

A. I can't determine positively, but for months.

Q. Was it open at the time the child was taken to Dr. Parker -- the same wound from the operation ?

A. Yes, sir.

Q. Was it open at the time the child was examined by Dr. Carnochan ?

A. Yes, sir.

Cross-examined by Judge McKeon :

Q. How long have you lived in this city ?

A. In this city ? well, I should think, altogether, about 15 or 18 years.

Q. Have you been a physician all that time ?

A. Most of the time—yes, sir.

Q. Fifteen or eighteen years ?

A. Yes, sir.

Q. How much of the time ?

A. About 10 or 11 years I have practiced medicine in this city.

Q. What was your business prior to your entering upon the practice of medicine ?

A. A druggist.

Q. Where did you do business as a druggist ?

A. 703 Greenwich Street, the latter part of the time.

Q. Where else ?

A. Well, a number of different stores I was in : I served my time with Wm. N. Gilchrist, 62½ Spring Street.

Q. Where else ?

A. Benjamin Quackenbush, 703 Greenwich Street.

Q. Where else ?

A. That is the only stores I have been in, I have said.

Q. Were you proprietor ?

A. No, sir.

Q. Clerk ?

A. Yes, sir.

Q. With whom did you study medicine ?

A. With whom ? Wm. N. Gilchrist and Fabius J. Hayward.

Q. In this city ?

A. One of them, and the other in North Carolina.

Q. When did you study ?

A. Whenever I got the chance.

Q. When did you study with Gilchrist ?

A. Well; 1849, and part of time 1850.

Q. When with the other physician ?

A. That was in North Carolina.

Q. When was that ?

A After I left New York.

Q. Well, but when was that ?

A. I think it was in 1852 or '53 : I did not study regularly with him, but still I was instructed occasionally by him, and had books from his library.

Q. In 1852 or 53 ?

A. Yes, sir.

Q. You did not study ?

A. No, sir; but was instructed and had books from him.

Q. In North Carolina ?

A. Yes, sir.

Q. How long were you there ?

A. The better part of my life.

Q. The better part of your life, then, was 1852 or 53 ?

A. No, sir ; I say I was the most part of my life there.

Q. How long were you with him in North Carolina ?

A. With whom ?

Q. With Hayward.

A. I was not with him at all.

Q. Then you did not study with him ?

A. I said I did not, but had books from his library.

Q. Where was he ?

A. He was in the country ; he practiced in Raleigh, North Carolina.

Q. Where did you study ?

A. At home.

Q. Where was your house ?

A. Raleigh, North Carolina.

Q. But not with him ?

A. Not with Dr. Hayward ; no, sir.

Q. What else were you doing there ?

A. I was superintendent of mills where they manufactured castor oil ; a very good article, too.

Q. How long did you remain there and had books from the doctor's office ?

A. I do not recollect.

Q. About how long ?

A. I have no recollections at all.

Q. It was in the years '52 and '53 was it ?

A. I had them probably after that.

Q. To the best of your recollection ?

A. I have no recollection of it when I did, sir.

Q. Your memory has become pretty poor?

A. Not very poor; I think I recollect most things.

Q. Well, when you left Raleigh where did you go to?

A. I went to a good many places.

Q. Well, mention several of them.

A. I decline to answer the question; I decline to answer questions of that kind, because I consider them perfectly useless.

Q. Why do you decline to answer?

A. Because I consider it quite unnecessary; I am not to be examined in regard to my history, but in regard to any question of injury.

MR. CROAK: I object to that—it is quite proper.

By Judge McKEAN:

Q. When did you leave Raleigh?

A. What time do you mean?

Q. I want you to state that.

A. I do not recollect, but immediately previous to the war.

Q. But you do not recollect what year?

A. Yes, sir; the last time I was in Raleigh was just about the time that Fort Sumter was first—not Sumter, but Fort Moultrie, evacuated and Sumter taken charge of.

Q. Can you remember when that was?

A. It was in 1862.

Q. About that year that Fort Sumter was taken?

A. No, sir; Fort Moultrie was evacuated and Sumter taken charge of.

Q. By the United States troops?

A. No, sir; Moultrie was evacuated by the United States troops and they went over to Fort Sumter.

Q. You think that was in 1862?

A. I do not think anything about it because I do not know; I only know that I was in Raleigh immediately previous to that time.

Q. You refer to the time when the United States troops left Moultrie and went over to Sumter ?

A. Yes, sir.

Q. You think it was in 1862 ?

A. I do not think anything about it, because I have not charged my memory ; I was in Raleigh immediately previous to that time.

Q. And you left Raleigh just before the war ?

A. Yes, sir.

Q. And that is the time you refer to ?

A. Yes, sir; my mother died and I was telegraphed to.

Q. Do you remember the month of the year when the troops went over to Fort Sumter ?

A. No, sir.

Q. You think it was in 1862 ?

A. I do not think anything about it; I only know it was about the time.

Q. Why don't you know anything about it: because your memory is bad ?

A. No ; because I have not charged my memory particularly ; I only recollect the circumstance, and from what I heard ; there was a good deal of excitement when I was there.

Q. When you left Raleigh, North Carolina, where did you go to ?

A. I came to New York.

Q. Have you been back there since ?

A. I have been to North Carolina ; I have been within the lines, but not to Raleigh.

Q. When did you last have books from Mr. Hayward ?

A. I don't recollect.

Q. It was some time before this last time you left Raleigh, was it not ?

A. Yes, sir.

Q. From the time you ceased taking books from Mr. Hayward's office—

A. I did not take them ; I merely borrowed them as a friend.

Q. I did not mean that you stole them, but from the time you ceased borrowing books from Mr. Hayward until you left Raleigh, what business were you doing?

A. I told you that I was Superintendent of the Neuse River Oil Mills.

Q. Up to the time when you left Raleigh finally, you had studied only from the books you had from Dr. Hayward, or had you previously studied?

A. I had previously studied here, in New York, of course.

Q. With Dr. Gilchrist?

A. With Dr. Gilchrist.

Q. Where was his office?

A. 62½ Spring Street at the time.

Q. How long were you with Dr. Gilchrist?

A. I do not recollect the time.

Q. To the best of your recollection?

A. Probably altogether two years, may be.

Q. Were you in the office with him?

A. Yes, sir.

Q. In what capacity?

A. I was a clerk in the store.

Q. In the drug store?

A. Yes, sir; and had the advantages of his books.

Q. And it was his drug store?

A. Yes, sir; first his brother and then Dr. Gilchrist had it.

Q. Was the Doctor a practising physician at that time?

A. Yes, sir.

Q. At that time?

A. Yes, sir.

Q. Where was his office?

A. 62½ Spring Street.

Q. You attended to the drugs?

A. Yes, sir.

Q. And kept the books?

A. There are not generally any books kept in a drug store; I kept the prescription book, so far as pasting in the book the prescriptions was concerned.

Q. Well, Doctor, where else, or with whom else have you studied.

A. I did not come here to answer.

Mr. James : Oh, yes ; answer it.

Witness : I am not in any condition, and I am not going to answer any more questions in regard to that ; if any man doubts the fact of my being a regular physician, or my standing among physicians of New York, I can give them evidence of the fact ; I am not going to answer questions in regard to that point ; I am very unwell.

Q. It is just this evidence as—

A. Yes, sir. Well, I will answer no more questions in regard to that.

Q. With whom else, if anybody, have you studied medicine ?

A. I told you I will answer no more questions on that point.

Judge McKean : Well, I will take the ruling of the Referees.

Mr. Traphagen : It is a perfectly proper question.

By Judge McKean :

Q. Have you ever studied with any one else ?

A. Except my own reading, and when I was in the neighborhood of a doctor ; my condition in a pecuniary point of view was not such as to allow me to go and study without my labor. I received instructions from any physician I wanted.

Q. Have you ever attended a medical college as a student ?

A. Yes, sir.

Q. Where ; what ?

A. I have attended a good many lectures at college.

Q. Now state what medical college you have attended ?

A. Well, I am not going to answer any question of that kind.

Q. I ask you if you have attended medical colleges or classes ?

A. I have attended lectures at a number.

Q. Well now, doctor, just tell me what medical colleges you have attended.

A. I refuse to answer.

Mr. TRAPHAGEN : We all think it is perfectly proper that this . question should be answered by you; you have given your opinion as a medical man, and, of course, they have a right to know upon what it is based and what knowledge you have to give an opinion, and so the question is perfectly proper.

Mr. ESTES : The evidence is out and it is the question what it is worth.

WITNESS : I would rather not answer the question ; I decline to answer the question.

Dr. SWINBURNE : All the counsel want is to get at the fact as to how competent you are to judge on a question of this kind.

WITNESS : It is, in my opinion, not such a question, because I did not use my judgment; I went to those in a position to do so.

By Mr. SHAFER :

Q. You say you did not use your judgment ?

A. No, no ; I did not say that at all.

Mr. JAMES : I am not objecting to the question ; I think he is obliged to answer.

WITNESS : I do not pretend to be an expert; the difference between the fluid and other fluids in the body is so great that it would be very difficult to mistake, that is simply the point; it is not on my own decision in regard to it ; I relied more than on the decision of others.

By Judge McKEAN :

Q. You do not claim to be an expert ?

A. No, and I do not decide such to be the case now ; to confirm or reverse my judgment, I took the patient to others upon whom I put more confidence.

Dr. Swinburne : If you will answer the question simply, what advantages have you had ?

By Judge McKean :

Q. Then you mean to say, as a medical man and expert, that it was synovial fluid ?
A. To the best of my belief it was.
Q. And yet you do not claim to be an expert ?
A. No more than any one else who has studied the appearance.
Q. Now we will come back to the point of departure, about these colleges ; name one institution ?
A. I decline to answer.
Q. Though the Referees have twice held the question is proper, you refuse to answer ?

Mr. Estes : The evidence is not for the purpose of casting any odium, but for the purpose of ascertaining the extent of his knowledge and what his opinion is worth. I thought, perhaps, he might misunderstand the motive under which the question is asked.

By Judge McKean :

Q. Now I will try a new tack ; from what institution, Doctor, did you receive your diploma ?
A. It is the same question over again ; I decline to answer.

Mr. Traphagen : We give him the same instruction that he should answer.

Judge McKean : It is not my purpose to ask for very stringent proceedings against the witness, I only want to get at the truth, and if I can get at it by his refusal to answer, I am satisfied.

Q. Doctor, I ask where you said you lived at the time of going to see the little girl after the operation ?

A. I lived in Greenwich Street; I think it was, to the best of my recollection, 703.

Q. Have you any doubt about that?

A. I have no doubt, if I can recollect exactly the time; I have lived in the same neighborhood, or within several houses of the same neighborhood.

Q. Do you remember the year when the operation was performed?

A. I have answered that question, I think?

Q. Will you repeat it; I do not think you stated the year: what year was it the operation was performed; how many years ago?

A. I do not know the exact time the operation was performed.

Q. 1865, '66, '67, '68, or when?

A. I think May will be about two years since the operation was performed, if I mistake not.

Q. You think it might be two years since the operation was performed?

A. About that time.

Q. You lived in Greenwich Street. Where did you live before that?

A. Before I lived in 703 Greenwich Street?

Q. Yes; where did you last live before that?

A. 275 West Tenth Street.

Q. When was that?

A. It is an impossibility to tell; but my headquarters have been at 703 Greenwich Street.

Q. What do you mean by headquarters?

A. Well, there I directed calls to be made, and I have lived in the immediate neighborhood.

Q. How long have you kept your slate there, and called it your headquarters?

A. For ten or eleven years.

Q. Are you a man of family?

A. I am, sir.

Q. How much of a family?

A. I have a wife and three children living in the city.

Q. In the city?

A. Yes, sir; in the city.

Q. Where did you live before you lived in West Tenth Street; where did you live last before that?

A. 703 Greenwich Street I told you, sir.

A. No; that was after; I asked you before you lived there, and you said 275 West Tenth Street.

A. No; that was before that.

Q. Where did you live before you resided at 275 West Tenth Street?

A. 722 Greenwich.

Q. Where before that?

A. That was my first residence in the city—no, sir; I lived at the corner of Horatio Street and Eighth Avenue; I lived there a couple of months.

Q. Where did you live next after 703 Greenwich Street?

A. I did not live anywhere after that until I went to Tenth Street, on account of some alterations in the house.

Q. How long did you live there?

A. Not quite a year.

Q. Where did you go then?

A. I went to 596 Hudson Street.

Q. How long did you stay there, doctor?

A. I don't know the length of time I remained.

Q. About how long?

A. I remained there, I think, about a year; I am not sure in regard to that point.

Q. Where did you go then?

A. To 696 Greenwich Street, where I reside now.

Q. How long have you been there?

A. Since January or February last: I have had my office there for some time: since October, I think, or November.

Q. Where does the plaintiff live?

A. He lives at the corner of Charlton and Washington Streets.

Q. Has he some sort of a store in the building in which he lives?

A. He did have, I don't know anything to the contrary.

Q. It is a liquor shop?

A. It was, sir.

Q. Whisky grocery?

A. I believe they call it a porter house; it is not a grocery.

Q. They sell all kinds of liquor?

A. I do not know anything about it.

Q. Don't you drink?

A. I am a Son of Temperance, and have been for over a year.

Q. What were you before that?

A. What do you mean by that?

Q. Well, that is for you to say?

A. Well, I have tried to be an honest man?

Q. What in regard to your habits; did you drink then?

A. Yes, sir.

Q. How often?

A. It depended on how often I felt like it.

Q. What was your particular toddy?

A. I had no particular choice.

Q. You took all kinds?

A. I had no particular choice.

Q. Name them?

A. No, sir, I will not name them at all: I consider it entirely unnecessary to name them.

Q. Drank whisky, brandy, gin and so on?

A. I did not drink gin, because I did not require it.

Q. But the other drinks you occasionally indulged in?

A. I did, sir; I am very sorry to say.

Q. And that was while you were the family physician of this family.

A. Yes, part of the time.

Q. Well, in those days did you drink at Mr. Walsh's?

A. Sometimes, but it was very seldom I drank any kind of strong liquor at Mr. Walsh's more than a glass of ale.

Q. Took the strong liquors somewhere else?

A. Well, I never took much strong liquor; I should have

been willing to drink his strong liquor, but I preferred to drink ale.

Q. Are you a practising surgeon as well as physician?

A. No, sir; I generally get Dr. Sayre to perform my operations.

Q. What where the operations you got Dr. Sayre to perform?

A. Oh, well, I sent him a number of patients.

Q. Who?

A. I cannot remember; I had him operate upon a patient of mine one time after this by the name of Easton.

Q. What was the operation?

A. It was the opening of what was supposed by the doctor to be a deep-seated abscess.

Q. Where?

A. In the calf of the leg; he did not operate, but explored and found that it was so deep-seated that he could not determine positively in regard to it; he introduced a trocar and allowed the fluid to escape.

Q. How long was it after the operation on the little girl?

A. It was a long time before that.

Q. Who else beside Easton did you send to Dr. Sayre to operate upon?

A. I sent him a patient not a great while ago.

Q. Who was it?

A. I do not recollect.

Q. About how long ago?

A. Three or four months ago.

Q. You gave him Dr. Sayre's address and told him to call on him for an operation?

A. Yes, sir.

Q. A patient?

A. Well, they came from the country, and I sent them to Dr. Sayre.

Q. What was the difficulty with him?

A. Very similar to what I supposed—

Q. A deep-seated abscess?

A. No, sir; the hip joint.

Q. Very similar to the little girl's ?

A. Very similar in appearance ; I did not examine the patient at all.

Q. Well, do you remember any others besides these ?

A. Yes, sir ; I do recollect one other, I think ; when Dr. Sayre's office was on Broadway I took a patient there from Thirtieth Street, if I mistake not—a little girl.

Q. How long ago ?

A. It may be five or six years ago; they live in Thirtieth Street; it was a disease very similar to the little girl's.

Q. Do you know, Doctor, of any operation that Dr. Sayre performed on Mr. Walsh, the guardian of the plaintiff ?

(Objected to by Mr. CROAK.)

Mr. TRAPHAGEN : If objected to we cannot allow it.

Judge McKEAN : We offer to prove that he performed an operation for cancer.

Mr. SHAFER : And we go a little further, and say that he was supposed to be a pauper patient, but subsequently it was ascertained that he was a man of means and a charge of $100 was made. We supposed that this witness got the money, but failed to pay Dr. Sayre. An action was brought against Walsh, and instead of Walsh paying the money this witness came and compromised. We can also show that subsequently to this a conspiracy, on the part of the plaintiff and the witness, was entered into to institute the action in consequence of the prosecution against Walsh.

(Objection by Mr. CROAK.)

Mr. TRAPHAGEN : We exclude it.

(Exception taken by Judge McKEAN.)

By Judge McKean :

Q. Was this operation on the right or left side of the little girl?

A. On the right side.

Q. Are you sure it was on the right side?

A. To the best of my recollection.

Q. Now where is the hip joint; just explain, if you please?

A. I do not know what you mean by the hip joint; it is the union of the thigh bone with the bones of the pelvis, one having a ball and the other having a socket, as you would call it.

Q. Put your hand upon it, on your own person.

(Witness did so.)

Q. Well now, Doctor, how many ligaments has this hip joint?

A. What do you mean by ligaments? What I mean is that which covers over the joint; it is an impossibility for me, in my present state, to go into the complete anatomy of the joint; but there are other Doctors who will be here who can be examined on these points.

Q. To the best of your recollection, Doctor, how many ligaments are there connected with this hip joint?

A. I cannot name them at present; I do not say I could not tell them; I do not recollect all, so as to go into a minute description of the anatomy, at all.

Q. Mention some of the ligaments connected with the joint?

A. I cannot remember any of them at all; I hope, gentlemen, that this examination will be made only what you are obliged to, as I am very unwell; I shall ask to have the case adjourned; I came here against the advice of my physician.

Q. If I understand you aright, you cannot mention any of the ligaments connected with the hip joint?

Mr. Traphagen : He has said so.

By Judge McKean :

Q. Not one of them?

A. The joint is covered, for the joint contains this fluid.

Q. Well, how much fluid does it contain, about?

A. Well, I don't know exactly.

Q. In its natural state, I mean?

A. I think from 2 to 4 drachms at the farthest, if I mistake not.

Q. Well, what is the chemical composition and microscopic appearance of the healthy synovial fluid?

A. I could not give that—the microscopic appearance; it is a perfectly clear and transparent fluid.

Q. You cannot give the chemical composition of it?

A. No, sir; I cannot.

Q. You did not subject this fluid which you discovered in this child to a microscopic or chemical examination?

A. I did not, sir.

Q. Did you subject it in any instance?

A. I do not recollect that I ever did.

Q. Can you tell the difference between the synovial fluid and serous discharge from an inflamed ulcer?

A. Yes, sir; I think I could.

Q. What is the difference?

A. They difference in appearance generally; they are not of the same color, as a general thing.

Q. Wherein do they differ in color?

A. Well, one is more dark.

Q. Which is darker?

A. It is not always darker, but it is generally of a straw color.

Q. The synovial fluid is not always darker?

A. It is mostly of a straw color, as I would call it.

Q. But it is not always darker?

A. Not always darker, because one is perfectly transparent, and one is not.

Q. What is a serous discharge; what do you mean by serum, or serous discharge?

A. I mean by serous discharge the same as you would get from a blister, or something of that kind.

Q. Describe it?

A. I do not know that I can describe it particularly; if you put a blister on at night and take a microscope to-morrow, and examine it—

Q. I ask you as a scientific man?

A. I do not pretend to be such, as far as a microscope is concerned.

Q. But as a medical man, what is serum; what does it come from; what is its origin?

A. It must be inflammation, of course, and congestion of the parts; when you put a blister on—

Q. What is it in nature; how does it arrive; what part of the system does it come from; from the bone, or how?

A. It must come from the blood.

Q. What is it?

A. Well, that I cannot explain.

Q. Can you tell the difference between the synovial fluid and the sanious discharge from a chronic abscess, without making a microscopic examination?

A. That question I could not answer.

Q. What is a sanious discharge?

A. It is generally a very acrid matter that is discharged from unhealthy sores and wounds of any kind.

Q. How does it arrive; what part of the system does it come from?

A. Well, I do not know that I can give you a full explanation of that.

Q. What is the difference between a serous and sanious discharge?

A. I am not prepared to go into an explanation of that point.

Q. Then you cannot tell?

Mr. CROAK: I object.

Q. Then you cannot tell?

A. I might probably be able to tell, but I am not positive.

Q. You cannot tell now?

A. Not at this present moment.

Q. Can you, then, tell me, putting it in one question, can you tell me the difference between the synovial and serous and sanious discharge ?

A. The synovial fluid, as I have been taught, has no appearance ?

Q. As you have been taught ?

A. It is an impossibility for me to go into the particular difference, that is, the chemical difference.

Q. Can you decide between them without chemical or microscopic examination ?

A I think I might; but if the question was involved I should call somebody more qualified to judge ; that is a point, if I had any doubts, I should call in Dr. Sayre or Dr. Parker to tell me.

Q. Then you do not feel qualified to decide that point ?

A. I do not say that I am not qualified to answer the question at all, but I am not now prepared.

By Mr. SHAFER :

Q. Do you feel now competent to decide ?

A. No ; not to go into a full description ; I am not physically capable

Q. Did you, when you saw this little girl after the operation by Dr. Sayre the first time, or any time, examine by the microscope, or chemically, the fluid you saw discharging from the abscess ?

A. I did not, sir.

By Dr. SWINBURNE :

Q. I understand the Doctor has paid special attention to the subject of medicine, but not to anatomy or surgery, but I would like to know how much he knows of anatomy ?

A. Well, I am not fully posted in regard to anatomy, I know no more than the generality of other practitioners who live in large cities.

Judge McKean : The Doctor did say that he did not consider himself a surgeon.

By Dr. Swinburne :

Q. He may be a physiologist and not understand surgery ; I would like to know where the wound was that he discovered—in what precise position as regards the hip joint ?

A. The opening do you mean ?

Q. Yes, the opening.

A. It was almost over the union where the ball—

Q. Where your thumb is now ?

A. Yes ; there seemed to be two operations ; the trocar had been introduced once above and once below.

Q. Do you know the depth of the hip joint from the surface ?

A. I do not, exactly—it could not be a great distance.

Q. Do you remember the opening, whether it went up and down or transversely ?

A. I think it was up and down, or had the appearance of it.

Q. How deep was the opening ; did you discover ?

A. I did not probe the opening ; of course, if the synovial fluid was escaping, it must have indicated the joint.

Q. Have you seen the discharge which comes from a bursa ; did you ever see the fluid that comes from an enlarged bursa ?

A. It appeared more like a straw color where there is no pus at all.

Q. Was this from the bursa or not ; it was not from the line of the shaft itself ?

A. No, sir.

Q. Anterior or posterior, or which ?

A. On a direct line.

Q. Posterior or anterior to the line of the shaft of the femur ?

A. It was just about that point—just where the working of the joint would interfere.

Q. You have not studied pathology ?

A. I did, to a certain extent ; I have not studied pathological anatomy.

John F. Walsh called. Examined by Mr. Croak :

Q. You know Dr. Sayre ?

A. Yes. sir.

Q. How long have you known him ?

A. About two or three years.

Q Are you the father of Margaret Sarah Walsh ?

A. Yes, sir,

Q. Please state if there was something the matter with your daughter, Margaret Sarah Walsh.

A. There appeared to be, sir.

Q. To whom did you take, or who attended her first ?

A. I directed her to be taken to Dr. Sayre.

Q. Was she taken there ?

A Yes ; to get his advice and see what was the trouble with her ; the mother took the child there, and she informs me—

(Objection.)

By Mr. Traphagen :

Q. Were you present at the time ?

A. No, sir ; I am speaking what my wife told me.

By Mr. Croak :

Q. Did you take the child to see Dr. Parker ?

A. Yes, sir ; several times.

Q. What was done the first time ?

A. The first time Dr. Parker examined the child he said—

(Objection. Allowed.)

Q. What did Dr. Parker direct you to do ?

(Objection. Allowed.)

Q. You are appointed guardian of the child ?

A. Yes, sir.

Judge McKean : We waive the objection as to what Dr. Parker said.

By Mr. Croak :

Q. Well, what did Dr. Parker say ?
A. He said it was synovial fluid that ran from the hip joint.

By Mr. Shafer:

Q. You say that Dr. Parker punctured the hip joint ?
A. No, sir.

By Mr. Croak :

Q. What were the exact words ?
A. He said, after he examined the child, that it was synovial fluid that was running, and that the child was very weak and ill, and had to be got out of that and strengthened up, and he prescribed some medicine, and so forth, and directed me, I think he said, to have a wagon made, so that she would not be on the foot, and I did so ; I had a wagon made to wheel her around the streets ; he advised me to take her into the country, to Rockaway, and I did so ; and then, after we came back, he advised me to take her to another part of the country, to Fort Washington, and there she was for five or six weeks ; and then we went to Jersey, for two or three weeks.

Q. What did the wagon cost you ?

(Objection. Allowed.)

Q. How long did she remain in the country ?
A. She was in the country most of the summer, between Rockaway, Jersey, and Fort Washington.

Q. When did Dr. Carnochan call ?
A. It was about a couple of weeks after.

Q. Did you tell Dr. Parker that there had been an operation performed ?

A. Not until after he had expressed his opinion ; when I fetched the child in, I said that I had a sick child to be examined; I did not tell him there was an operation performed; when he stripped the child he said the hip joint had been opened, and that was synovial fluid.

Q. When did you see Dr. Carnochan?

A. I think it was about a week or two after that; the child was not getting any better, and I thought I would try Dr. Carnochan, as I heard about his being a first-class doctor, able to cure anything, and I sent for Dr. Carnochan to come to the house, and Dr. Vaughan was in the room at the time and me, and the Doctor came in, and he asked what was the matter; I said there is a sick child.

Mr. Shafer: We regard this evidence incompetent, but in a spirit of liberality we allow him to go on and state what anybody said to him. We are so satisfied the truth is with us that he can go on and make his statement.

Witness: I says, I have got a sick child, and I sent for you to examine the child, and he looked at it, and he says: this joint has been opened to the hip, and he held something on his finger and says this is synovial fluid running out; well, he says, it is pretty bad, that child is pretty well weakened down—reduced: well, the two doctors talked among themselves; they did not tell me, of course; I asked them what the consequence was.

By Mr. Gage:

Q. You speak of Dr. Carnochan?

A. Yes, Dr. Carnochan; Dr. Parker was not at the house, every time we took the child to Dr. Parker's house, and I think I asked him what the consequence would be, and the reply was, that it would be crippled for life or either kill the child; to the best of my knowledge that was the reply.

Mr. Croak: Do I understand you, that in the same spirit of liberality, you will allow us to put in the order at any time— Mr. James has taken the papers with him.

Mr. Gage: We will allow it at any time.

Cross-examined by Judge McKean :

Q. How long had the little girl been ill before Dr. Sayre performed the operation ?

Q. Well, sir, I do not know ; I never noticed anything the matter with her, except I happened to notice one day she walked a little lame.

Q. How long was this before ?

A. A week or two.

Q. The first you noticed ?

A. Yes, sir, for I ain't in the house much ; it might have been a week ; I do not think it was more than that.

Q. Did the little girl sustain a fall some months before that ?

A. I heard—I say I don't know.

Mr. CROAK : Go on.

A. I heard that the child was in the hall-way and a baby wagon, and that she fell over that.

By Judge McKEAN :

Q Some time before ?

A. Some months ; I could not tell whether it was two weeks or seven months.

Q. And you heard from the mother ?

A. I can't say I heard from `her—from somebody in the house.

Q. Did you understand that the fall hurt her ?

A. Yes.

Q. Did you hear where it hurt her ?

A. No, sir ; I did not.

Q. When you went to Dr. Parker did Dr. Parker probe the wound ?

A. No, sir.

Q. Did he make any microscopic examination ?

A. I don't think he did any more than examine with the naked eye.

Q. Did he take the fluid and subject it to any chemical test ?

A. Not that I know of; I don't think he did ; no, sir, he did not.

Q. Did he put anything in the wound at all ?

A. I think not.

Q. How long was it after this that you took her to Dr. Carnochan ?

A. I didn't take her

Q. Called him to her ?

A. I think it was a couple of weeks.

Q. After she had been to Dr. Parker ?

A. Yes, sir.

Mr. TRAPHAGEN : Do we understand that both cases are pending ; are we trying both ?

Mr. CROAK : So I understand it.

Mr. ESTES : What is the point in the other case ?

Judge McKEAN : We don't consider that both are on trial.

Mr. SHAFER : There is a suggestion we desire to make : if this case—the case by this infant to recover damages personally —should be decided against us, that decides the other question against us and so it would be competent to go into special damages ; we think that that should be withheld until the main question is decided.

Mr ESTES : I got the impression from Mr. James and the opposite counsel that both questions were to be tried together.

Mr. GAGE : It was suggested by Mr. James that both should be tried together ; I said that, Mr. Shafer not being present, we did not feel disposed to consent to that until after a consultation with Mr. Shafer.

Mr. SHAFER : The plaintiff makes up a claim of five or six

hundred dollars for money expended, etc. ; if we should dispose
of the point by a trial, we should take two or three days more ;
the point we make is that the question respecting this amount
of money shall be reserved upon the condition that if you be
against us, then we go into that; we can only be held liable on
the ground of misconduct and negligence, so it is understood
that the case be reserved.

Mr. Croak : I would wish to consult with Mr. James.

By Judge McKean :

Q. When Dr. Carnochan was called to the little girl what examination did he make ?

A. Well, he stripped the child and made the same kind of
examination Dr. Parker made.

Q. Did he introduce any instrument ?

A. No, sir.

Q. Did he put any fluid in it ?

A. No, sir ; not that I know of.

Q. Did he take a microscope and examine the wound or
discharge ?

A. Not that I saw.

Q. Went through with no chemical experiments ?

A. No, sir.

Q. Well, Mr. Walsh, did not your wife take the little girl a
long time before this operation, some months before this operation, to Dr Sayre for examination ?

A. No, sir.

Q. Did not ?

A. No, sir.

Q. Not to your knowledge, or do you know positively she
did not ?

A. I do not think she did ; she never saw Dr. Sayre only
once.

Q. You were here the other day when your wife testified, and
heard her testimony ?

A. Yes, sir.

By Mr. Shafer:

Q. You swear she did not then testify—you swear that she did not state she had been there?

A. I do not think she did.

Q. Will you swear she did not so state?

A. To the best of my knowledge?

Q. Are you clear, are you positive she did not, are you certain and positive she did not so state?

A. I don't think she did.

Q. If she did so state, it has escaped your memory?

A. Yes, sir.

Mr. Croak: Dr. Parker was here and said that he could not be here until Wednesday of next week again.

Mr. Shafer: We know that next month is vacation, and that this is a very busy month in the profession, and the medical gentlemen are going to Europe in July. Dr. Parker was here, to my certain knowledge, and the counsel should not have taken the liberty of saying that he could go.

Mr. Croak: It has been no arrangement of mine.

Mr. Shafer: Dr. Carnochan is at Staten Island.

Dr. Swinburne: I said that I was willing to please you legal gentlemen, and could stay for these three days, as I wished to finish up the case, so that I could go away. Dr. Parker was here to-day, but the gentlemen allowed him to go off.

Mr. Croak: Well, I expect to be ready to-morrow.

Mr. Traphagen: Is there any reason why you should not be ready for to-morrow?

Mr. Shafer: We shall insist strictly to-morrow, if Dr. Parker is not here, that he is absent by their *laches*, in allowing the Doctor to leave, Mr. James having given him permission. We shall insist that, if he or the other witnesses are not here, their case shall be closed.

Mr. GAGE: It was understood in my office, yesterday, that they would close their case this week—that was so understood.

Judge McKEAN: It was understood that these three days should be devoted to the case, and certainly it was remarkable that Mr. James should have allowed the Doctor to go.

Mr. TRAPHAGEN to Mr. Walsh: It will be necessary for you to show very strong evidence that you endeavored to subpœna the witnesses, or be held to a very strict account; these persons can probably be subpœnaed to-day.

Adjourned to next day, June 3, 1870, at 3 P. M.

SUPERIOR COURT.

MARGARET SARAH WALSH, an infant, by
JOHN F. WALSH, her guardian,

against

LEWIS A. SAYRE.

June 3, 1870.

Before W. E. TRAPHAGEN, Esq., Dr. SWINBURNE, and BENJ.
ESTES, Esq., Referees.

Dr. PARKER, sworn and examined by Mr. JAMES :

Q. Your first name is Willard ?

A. Yes, sir.

Q. You are a surgeon and physician ?

A. Yes, sir, both ; I have acted in the capacity of both.

Q. Do you remember the child Margaret Sarah Walsh, the
daughter of the plaintiff ?

A. I do, sir.

Q. Do you remember when it was she came to you ?

A. I have not the precise date, but it was either the last of
May or 1st of June, in 1868, two years ago.

Q. Do you remember who brought her to you, Dr. Parker ?

A. Well, the mother and a physician, a gentleman by the
name of Vaughan ; but I am not quite sure whether the father
was present at that time or not ; my impression is that he was
not.

Q. Did you examine the child ?

A. I did.

Q. I want to ask you *what* (that would not be strictly) but
was something told you about the child having submitted to an
operation ?

A. The child was brought into my examining room, and I

think Dr. Vaughan made the remark; I did not know Dr.
Vaughan, he introduced himself; the question was whether it
was hip disease, that was the question; I examined the child
by stripping her and placing her upon a couch; I examined the
limbs with a view to ascertain whether there was any disease in
the hip joint or not; I came to the conclusion that there was no
disease in the hip joint, and so stated. In making my examination, and passing my hands around the buttocks, I came
in contact with a liquid, and I enquired what that meant, and
then it was stated to me by the mother—

(Objection.)

Witness continuing—I discovered this liquid upon the buttocks; I asked what was the meaning of this.

Judge McKean : I object to what the mother said.

Mr. James: Then I submit the matter to the Referees; it is
a part of the *res gestae*, it is a statement accompanying the act;
it has never been disputed by Dr. Sayre that he performed an
operation—whether skillfully or not, it remains for your honors
to decide.

Judge McKean : We do not wish to argue such a question as
that; we simply object to the evidence as improper and inad-
missible.

Mr. Traphagen : That is the opinion of the Court; however,
they think it would be better to take the testimony and consider
it, giving no more weight to it than it is worth; we do not consider it competent as a question of law.

(Exception.)

By Mr. James :
Q. State what occurred ?
A. She then stated the fact that she had taken the child to

the office of Dr. Sayre, and that Dr. Sayre had there used an instrument, a needle, as I understood her to say, and had plunged it several times into that region, and she further stated her protestations against so doing, and so on; that was all she said; then Dr. Vaughan and myself retired, with a view to consultation and advice, to another room.

Q. I need hardly ask you if you made a careful examination of the child?

A. I did, sir; yes, sir.

Q. Now, with reference to the synovial fluid, will you state what you actually saw at the time?

A. There was a certain amount of fluid that I discovered on the region of the buttocks, just behind the hip joint; that fluid was glairy and viscid; that is all I know about it; whether it was synovial fluid or not I cannot determine.

Q. Can you give any opinion as to what it was?

A. I could not, very definitely.

Q. To the best of your judgment?

A. I must confess that it passed my mind that he had passed the needle and reached the cavity of the hip joint; I knew nothing else; I simply found this fluid, and that was the matter that passed my mind; that is all: we then retired, as I said before, and advised on the course of treatment for the child, which course, I believe, was followed out.

Q. Did you feel the fluid?

A. I felt the fluid on the end of my finger, which arrested my attention; it was somewhat viscid.

Q. I want to know your opinion, before these gentlemen; in your judgment was that synovial or not?

Judge McKean: The Doctor has already given his opinion.

Mr. James: No, sir; I am perfectly entitled to it.

Judge McKean: I withdraw the objection.

By Mr. James :

Q. To the best of your judgment was that synovial fluid ?

A. From all the knowledge I suspected it to be synovial fluid.

Q. Is the synovial fluid—to a gentleman of your experience—is it detectable ?

A. I think not—not absolutely from other kinds of fluid. We have what are called bursa sacs, where you have a similar fluid ; you have it sometimes from an old abscess ; it is impossible, perhaps absolutely, by any means, to determine the one from the other ; but taking the several ones by a microscopic examination and chemical analysis, there would be shades of difference discovered, but nothing of that kind was done by me.

Q. Did you express at the time any opinion that it was synovial fluid ?

A. No, sir.

Q. Did you ever give that opinion ?

A. No, sir.

Q. From your judgment now, referring back to the date of your examination, in your judgment, was that synovial fluid or not ? I want your judgment.

A. I am unable to say definitely ; I say, from all the evidence before me at the time, I was led to favor the opinion that it was synovial fluid.

Q. What would be the effect upon the system of the discharge of synovial fluid ?

A. The effect immediately would not amount to much, but the subsequent effects may prove serious indeed, in the shape of an inflammation of the joint.

Q. Suppose that synovial fluid had been discharging from that wound for a period of two months antecedently to the child having been seen by you, would there be any palpable appearance on the joint or organization ?

A. Two months would have been likely to have produced active inflammation in the joint, unless the discharge closed up.

Q. What was the state of the wound ?

A. Nothing except a mere pin-hole, perhaps large enough to admit a probe.

Q. Then you can give nothing more accurate than that ?

A. No, sir.

Q. Your opinion was that it was—

A. No ; I did say that, in the absence of all other evidence, I suspected that it came from the cavity of the joint.

Q. That is the same thing ?

A. The same thing ; certainly, the same thing.

Q. Then you mean that your observation was not sufficiently accurate to enable you to express a positive opinion ?

A. I simply say that I could not give or would not give it as a positive opinion at all.

Q. Were there any appearances of sore or disease that would emit anything from the wound besides synovial fluid ?

A. I discovered nothing of the kind.

Q. That would have emitted fluid ?

A. I think not—nothing.

Q. How long was the child under examination ?

A. Well, perhaps ten minutes or so that I had the child stripped and was under my hands in the way of examination ; the child was in the office perhaps half an hour.

Q. Have you seen the child since ?

A. Yes, sir ; several times.

Q. Can you give us the dates ; was she brought to your house ?

A. I cannot ; the child was advised to the course by Dr. Vaughan and myself, to be taken into the country, to keep the joint entirely at rest and build up the system ; that was the direction ; the child was brought to me in the last of August or in the fore part of September, the precise time I am unable to state ; the child was at the office at that time, and the father and the mother, and I think Dr. Vaughan was also with the child, but I am not quite sure as to Dr. Vaughan.

Q. Did you ever examine the child after that examination ?

A. I examined it after that, and I found the condition of things confirmed my previous opinion that the hip joint was not diseased; the opening through which the fluid escaped was entirely closed, and there was no discharge from that region at all, and the result of our advice and treatment seemed to have been very satisfactory.

Q. When was the last time you saw the child?

A. I do not remember, but it might be six months, and it may be less or more.

Q. Was the child better or worse?

A. The child became very sick indeed after that—very.

Q. What are the symptoms, in your experience—the appearance of the hip joint—where the synovial fluid has been allowed to escape by any operation?

A. There would be no special appearance, provided the opening closed up in season; but if the opening remained and the discharge continued, inflammation is pretty sure to supervene a length on the membrane lining the cavity, and when that supervenes it produces very serious results in the shape of inflammation of the joint and displacement of the head of the bone, and a variety of that kind of thing.

Q. What is the date, about, of the last time you ever saw the child?

A. It may be six months, or more or less.

Q. Six months since?

A. Yes, sir.

Q. Then it would come to January of this year?

A. January or December of this year

Q. Will you state what you saw in the child about six months ago?

A. There was no difficulty about the hip joint at all.

Q. What state was she in?

A. She had extensive abscesses occurring about the body of the thigh and buttocks, and so on—pretty extensive abscesses, and her system had been very much borne down by inflammation and suppuration that was occurring.

Q. Had the child the perfect use of the hip joint when you saw her?

A. I think not a perfect use, there was more or less—there was no shortening, no displacement of the foot at all, but there was some defect in the motion generally, depending on the inflammation that had occurred.

Q. Could she walk when you saw her?

A. I think she could very well.

Q. Could she walk?

A. I think so, sir; I believe the child walked.

Q. Now you say you expressed an opinion at the time, or entertained an opinion; what was there in existence, in the state of the hip at that time, that could have produced any discharge such as you saw, unless it was the discharge of the synovial fluid?

A. I do not know that there was anything.

Q. When you examined her, you could see, I presume, where the puncture had been made by the probe or needle?

A. I could see the aperture through which the fluid was oozing.

Q. What was there that could have produced the discharge except it was the discharge of the synovial fluid; was there any other cause?

A. I knew nothing at that time.

Q. Suppose we take the operation to have been made about the 10th or 12th March, before you saw her in the latter end of April or so, had the orifice been open all that time?

A. It was open when it came to me.

Q. Well, what I want to understand is this—though you do not give a positive opinion, unless this was a discharge of the synovial fluid, what cause was existing to produce the discharge of any other fluid than that?

(Objection by Mr. Shafer).

(Overruled).

Question repeated, and further.

By Mr. JAMES:

Q. Did you discover any other cause that would produce the discharge of any other fluid than that?

A. All I discovered was simply this opening and this fluid escaping therefrom—that is all.

Q. I just want to repeat the question—it is not quite an answer to the question; did you discover any other cause that would produce the discharge of any other fluid?

Mr. SHAFER: He has gone over the ground to the utmost extent.

Mr. TRAPHAGEN: We do not think the last answer was directly in point.

WITNESS: I simply saw the aperture from whence this discharge came, it being situated over the region of the joint, and connecting that fact with the story I heard, I suspected strongly that it came from the cavity capsule of the joint; but yet it might have come from other sources, as I said before.

Mr. JAMES: I put it for the second time.

(Objection by Mr. Shafer.)

By Mr. JAMES:

Q. Will you name any other source from which that fluid could have come?

A. Had I introduced a probe into that aperture and carried that probe into the cavity of the joint, I could have answered your question very explicitly; if I had introduced the probe and carried it to another cavity, not the cavity of the joint, I could have made you another answer; I did not know there was any abscess; I heard nothing about the abscess, or any trouble, except the mere fact I have stated.

Q. Then you did not make a sufficient examination to form an opinion; or did you make a sufficient examination to find any other cause than that for the discharge of the synovial fluid ?

A. I did not go further; I deemed it bad surgery to go further; introducing an instrument would have brought about a state of things which we sought by treatment to avoid.

Q. Is the synovial fluid easily known by experienced surgeons ?

A. I think it is not; there are other fluids so nearly assimmilated to it that it would not be easy to determine.

Q. How would you detect it ?

A. If a given quantity of fluid was given to you, submit it to chemical and microscopical analysis.

Q. Then you say the fluid might be the discharge from what ?

A. The fluid might have come from an ulcer, or it might have come from an abscessal membrane for aught I know.

Q. How often did you see the child altogether ?

A. I should think I saw the child six or eight times.

Mr. JAMES : That is all I shall ask at present.

Judge McKEAN . I think there is no necessity for asking Dr. Parker any question.

Mr. TRAPHAGEN : We do not propose to be the judges of that.

Judge McKEAN : I mean for ourselves; if the Referees wish to ask any questions, of course they can do so.

By Dr. SWINBURNE :

Q. How long after the operation did you see the child ?

A. I don't know; I saw the child about two years ago now— the last of May or first of June, but how long that was after the child had been to Dr. Sayre's office I do not think I knew—I do not think I heard anything about that.

Q. What was the condition of that child—like one scrofulous ?

A. Yes, I should say the child was scrofulous.

Q. How long had the child been taking the syrups of iodide and of the phosphates?

A. Before I saw her.

Q. Yes?

A. I don't know.

Q. Will you be kind enough to tell us where the wound was?

A. It was half way between the trochanter major and tuber of the hip bone.

Q. How deep would that be?

A. To reach the capsule it would be an inch, or an inch and a half; the child was not in an emaciated condition; there was only a hitch in the gait; that was all visible when she came in the room.

Q. Our impression is that you stated it was opened by a needle?

A. It was stated that it was opened by an instrument thrust in that direction.

Q. Was it an exploring needle?

A. I suppose so; I had no means of judging.

Q. As a surgeon, what harm would result therefrom?

A. Inflammation would follow.

Q. Would it be the same if, when a stream of fluid poured out, a piece of fleshy matter came out as big as the end of the finger—what would you look upon that as?

A. It would be impossible, as connected with the joint.

Q. Would it look as if the fluid came from the joint?

A. No, sir; it would not.

Q. Suppose, the same evening, after the operation, you had seen the child and found the child had been operated upon, and you found, accidentally or otherwise— suppose you had found the fluid escaping in a stream, what would that indicate in your mind—that it was the joint open?

A. No, sir; it could not be.

Q. Well, here is another point that struck me with force: you say, all the way through, the hip joint is not diseased, and has not been?

A. As far as I have discovered, I have not referred the symptoms to an actual intracapsular disease at all.

Q. Suppose any needle or lancet had been used for opening the hip and the joint had been injured—if any mischief had followed, would you have abscesses outside the hip joint, if the injury was in the hip joint?

A. I think not, sir.

Q. Now you say that there was a viscid matter discharging, a considerable amount of it, and you say you have come—

A. No, I did not say that.

Q. There was some viscid matter?

A. My fingers came in contact with it.

Q. You did not examine it with the eye?

A. There was not enough of it.

Q. So that you could not tell the color?

A. No, sir.

Q. It might have come from a diseased bursa, or abscess?

A. From any secreting surface.

Q It might have come from a healthy bursa or diseased bursa, or from an abscess of scrofulous character?

A. Yes, sir.

Q. It would come of the same viscid character?

A. Yes, sir; understand, I heard nothing of abscess, I never knew of an abscess—I never knew of an abscess until the 21st day of November, of the same year.

Q. What I understand you to say is this—if the joint had been injured in the operation, and this abscess were the result of that injury, the joint would now, and would have been all the way through, involved more or less?

A. I should suppose so; certainly.

Mr. JAMES: There is a letter addressed to the Referees from Dr. Carnochan, in which he says he cannot attend to-day.

Mr. TRAPHAGEN: Have you any other witness?

Mr. JAMES: I want to call Dr. Carnochan first.

Mr. Traphagen : Have you others ?

Mr. James : One or two.

Mr. Traphagen : Can you call them now ?

Mr. James : No, sir.

Mr. Shafer : I am certain that one of the Court understands how easy it is to get from Staten Island to this place ; one of the members of the Court has occupied the same position, and to get a letter from Dr. Carnochan of this kind surprises us. Now we submit that unless Dr. Carnochan is here to-day, and unless they have subpœnaed other witnesses, your honors should require them to say that their case is closed.

Mr. James : I shall say nothing of the kind.

Mr. Traphagen : We have all considered that point and think it would be hardly fair for us to do so.

Mr. Shafer : I submit he should be attached.

Mr. James : Attach him on your own subpœna.

Mr. Shafer : Or on your own ; if they do not take an attach ment they should call their case closed.

Mr. Traphagen : We have concluded to meet to-morrow at 2 o'clock, and the plaintiff must have his witnesses ; they may take an attachment or other means ; it would not be fair to close the case as it now stands.

Mr. James : If we are not to have the usual justice in this ref- erence, I shall retire ; I cannot be ready to-morrow ; I don't think I can be here to-morrow.

Mr. Shafer : Let us understand ; if the counsel cannot be here to-morrow, I don't want to remain.

It was then agreed to adjourn until Tuesday next, at 3 P. M.

MARGARET SARAH WALSH, an infant, by
   JOHN F. WALSH, her guardian,
          against
   LEWIS A. SAYRE.

            Adjourned Reference
            Testimony — *June*
            7, 1870.

Dr. CARNOCHAN called and sworn for plaintiff:

Examined by Mr. JAMES:

Q. Do you remember the child, Margaret Sarah Walsh, in this suit?

A. Yes, I do.

Q. Was the child brought to you, Dr. Carnochan, or did you go to the house?

A. The first time, I believe—it is a good while since this occurred, but I think the first time—I was called to see the child was by Dr. Vaughan; he called at my office and asked me if I would meet him in consultation in the case of trouble about the hip joint; I said, certainly, and appointed a time.

Q. Do you remember about the time that it was, Doctor?

A. Well, I think, in 1868 some time; may be about November; I don't recollect; I took no memoranda about the case.

Q. Was it brought to your knowledge that it had undergone some operation?

A. I don't know that I talked anything about the case until I saw the child; I was in a hurry at the time when Dr. Vaughan called on me, and I think I appointed an hour to meet him, and parted from him.

Q. Now, do you recollect of the child being brought and your seeing the child?

A. Oh, I recollect seeing the child at the house of the parents.

Q. In Charlton Street?

A. I forget; I believe it was.

Q. Did you make an examination of the child?

A. I did make an examination, as is ordinarily done.

Q. Do you remember who were present?

A. Dr. Vaughan was present.

Q. And the parent—the father?

A. The parents both, I think, were present; I forget; the child was in a room that the parents were passing and repassing.

Q. Well, now, state what you found on examination, as well as you remember—the injured part and so on ; what part did you examine—the hip joint?

A. I examined the child generally—the child was in bed; of course my attention was directed to the part of the body that was supposed to be diseased, and I there examined the hip joint, more particularly the region of the hip ; do you wish me to go on or will you put questions to me?

Q. Describe it in your own way.

A. I remember seeing the orifice in the region of the hip—the posterior aspect of the hip, called the gluteal region ; probably you had better ask me questions.

Q. Well, did you examine any discharge of fluid that was coming from the orifice ; was your attention attracted by that?

A. Yes ; my attention was attracted by a discharge coming from the orifice?

Q. Was your attention attracted to the particular character of the discharge?

A. Yes.

Q. Well, what was it, to the best of your recollection?

A. It was a glairy fluid, slightly colored.

Q. I need hardly ask you the question—you are acquainted with the synovial fluid, the character and appearance of the synovial fluid?

A. Yes.

Q. In your judgment, did you find any synovial fluid discharging from that orifice?

A. It struck me so that it was.

Q. Did you examine it at all ?

A. I examined it with my fingers, and looked at its general tenacity, color, &c.

Q. Was that the opinion you formed at the time, as well as you remember ?

A. Yes.

Q. Did you state that opinion at the time ?

A. I think it is very likely I did.

Q. Was it brought, at the time, to your attention that the child had undergone some operation ?

A. Afterwards it was ; I suppose I asked some questions as to the wound, whether the orifice was natural or one made.

Q. What was about the size of the orifice, Dr. Carnochan ?

A. As far as I can recollect, it seemed to be towards half an inch or so in size ; it was not circular, it was rather longitudinal —rather longer than it was broad.

Q. Did you see the child more than once, Dr. Carnochan ?

A. Yes, I saw the child at intervals ; probably two or three times.

Q. Did you observe a discharge which you believed to be synovial fluid, upon any other occasion ?

A. I think the second time I saw the child it was dripping the same kind of fluid.

Q. What was your judgment as to the character of the fluid, the second time that you saw it ?

A. Well, my opinion at the time was that it was synovia fluid.

Q. Has anything occurred to alter your opinion from that you formed at the time ?

A. Well, I never thought the case of any consequence ; it was a matter of difficulty to know where the fluid came from, else than from where synovial fluid generally does come.

Q. Did you observe any cause, so far as your observation and examination went, to account for the discharge from that orifice of any fluid—any other than synovial fluid ?

A. I could not well account for it from any sources other than where the synovial fluid does come from.

Q. Was the orifice so placed, located, or situated, that a puncture would bring out—if done inexpertly it would bring out—synovial fluid; was the orifice so situated in reference to the joint?

A. Yes.

Cross-examined by Mr. Shafer :

Q. Was the hip joint diseased?

A. You mean when?

Q. At the time you saw it?

A. The hip joint did not—there were no particular indications that the hip joint was in a state of disease.

Q. Is there any disease that would occasion the flow of the synovial fluid from the hip joint?

A. No disease; just put the question again.

(Question repeated.)

A. Oh, yes.

Q. What diseases?

A. The hip joint, in certain times.

Q. You did not probe this wound?

A. No.

Q. Did you have any information whatever as to the condition of the child at the time it was at Dr. Sayre's?

A. No; not that I recollect.

Q. Had you any information that there was anything like a cold abscess?

A. No.

Q. If a cold abscess had existed, and been properly operated upon, would a discharge like that flow from it?

A. I do not think so.

Q. You think you can detect the synovial fluid without a microscope?

A. Yes.

Q. And without a chemical test?

A. Yes.

Q. Now state, if you can, the period or time when you saw the child?

A. I mentioned that I took no memoranda of the case; the case was brought to me in the latter part of the year; I don't suppose I thought of the case particularly in the interval; I think it was some time in 1868, about November.

Q. About November?

A. I am not sure.

Q. Are you sure the operation was performed in April, 1868?

A. I think I saw the case some three months after the operation had been done; I think I got that interval of time from a relative reasoning I have from the case; I did not think the case of much consequence, and I got rid of it.

Q. You thought it was cured?

A. I thought nothing of the kind.

Q. You did not think it was cured?

A. No.

Q. You did not think the case of much consequence?

A. In a professional sense; but to the child itself, it was.

Q. What do you mean by a professional sense?

A. Well, when a doctor has a number of cases, the fee, as regards it.

Q. Well, does the amount of fee that you receive make it of much consequence?

A. Well, I answer that, dwelling upon the word; that is a matter whether it is of consequence itself, or a matter of consequence relatively.

Q. Explain how?

A. Well, it is a matter of consequence to you whether you have an engagement up town.

Q. Explain how?

A. Well, a case may be of consequence if I am hurried; if I am not hurried it is not of consequence relatively, in time; that was in my mind as much as anything else.

Q. What was the condition of the child when you saw her—scrofulous?

A. It was very sick.

Q. Was it scrofulous?

A. Yes; it was a scrofulous child.

Q. Did you prescribe any treatment?

A. I prescribed the syrup of the iodide of iron, and something else; I forget.

Q. Will you be kind enough to show us where the wound was?

A. On what—if the child were here I could show you?

Q. Relatively?

A. I cannot, through your breeches.

Q. Relatively?

A. Well, it was an inch and a half from the trochanter major, from it internally—from an inch to an inch and a half; it is now a long time ago.

By Dr. Swinburne:

Q. From the interior?

A. From the trochanter—running from it.

By Mr. Shafer:

Q. How deep would it be from the hip joint?

A. That would depend on the condition of the child at the time; a fat or lean child would make a great deal of difference.

Q. Assuming it to be in its ordinary condition?

A. It was from an inch to two and a half.

Q. Would you go up or down to get into the hip joint from that point?

A. From which point?

Q. The point you described.

A. It was running from the trochanter.

Q. Now, if an operation was performed on the hip joint what would be the result?

A. What operation?

Q. If a hip joint was punctured by an exploring needle, what would be the result of the puncture?

A. Well, it may be one thing or another; the joints are opened with one result and then with another.

Q. Does inflammation follow ?

A. It does not necessarily follow.

Q. Does it ordinarily follow ?

A. It is apt to ; we take cartilages out of joints, and no inflammation follows, frequently ; and yet inflammation does follow.

Q. Now, suppose at the time this operation was performed by Dr. Sayre, a large stream of fluid poured out, and large pieces of fleshy matter came out, as big as the end of your finger, what would you look upon that as ?

A. I cannot suppose such a thing possible as that following a puncture.

Q. You know the incision was half an inch long ?

A. I don't know anything about the incision ; I say the puncture was about half an inch long.

Q. Suppose the operation was performed, and a stream of fluid came out and large pieces of fleshy matter as big as the end of your finger ?

A. I cannot look upon such a thing as possible ; it is not possible.

Q. Suppose, after the exploring needle was used, there was a slight appearance of matter, and then, upon the use of the bistoury, a stream of fluid poured out and pieces of fleshy matter came out, as big as the end of your finger, amounting to over a pint of fluid, what would you look upon that as ?

A. The fleshy matter came out ! I ask you if fleshy matter did come out ?

Q. Yes.

A. It is not possible.

Q. Why ?

A. Because it is not in the nature of things.

Q. Would an abscess produce such a thing ?

A. No ; mortified cellular tissue might; I suppose mortified cellular tissue could.

Q. Suppose there was the mortified tissue you have mentioned, and a discharge of matter, what would you call it ?

A. You speak as if an abscess was there.

Q. Would it indicate an abscess—that condition of things ?

A. Well, an abscess is a collection of purulent matter.

Q. The amount of matter would indicate an abscess ?

A. Well, after a pint of matter was exhausted it would be an abscess.

Q. Would such a quantity as we have described look as if coming from the hip joint ?

A. Yes; you see a hatful of matter come from a hip joint.

Q. Of synovial fluid ?

A. No, sir; such as you described.

Q. What quantity of synovial fluid would be discharged; suppose this hip joint was perfectly healthy, and no abscess was punctured there, what quantity of synovial fluid would come from such a puncture ?

A. There might be a teaspoonful come out.

Q. Would it secrete more than that ?

A. Yes; sometimes.

Q. What would be the maximum ?

A. A teaspoonful, or two, or three.

Q. Well, when you saw a hatful of matter, you mean a diseased hip joint, you don't mean a healthy hip joint ?

A. Not quite.

Q. Suppose the same evening after the operation, you saw the child, and find the child had been operated upon, and found fluid escaping in a stream—the evening after the operation, six or seven hours after the operation, you find a stream of matter escaping, such as this matter, would that indicate a hip disease or result of an abscess ?

A. The result of an abscess.

Q. It would not indicate that the hip had been opened ?

A. It depends on what stage of hip disease it was.

Q. This would not indicate that a healthy hip had been opened ?

A. No, sir; that there was disease of the character of a diseased hip; if such a condition of things were there it would indicate an abscess, or a collection of fluid—of matter.

Q. If the quantity of matter, I suppose, should come from a

hip joint, and diseased to that extent, it would have an effect upon the hip itself; would there be any mistaking of the hip disease ?

A. No, sir.

Q. The evidence of the disease would be unmistakable ?

A. Yes, sir.

Q. Suppose a needle or lancet had been used to open the hip, and the joint had been injured, or if any mischief had followed, would you have an abscess outside the hip joint, if the injury was in the hip itself ?

A. You may have an abscess following any puncture.

Q. But if the injury was to the hip joint itself, would you have an abscess form at a different point, and the hip get well ?

A. You may have an abscess follow a puncture, extending as low down as the hip joint; it might throw out synovial fluid and create an abscess.

Q. Would that disease be existing and the hip not be diseased, if it came from a puncture of the hip joint ?

A. The puncture might create an abscess.

Q. Would that affect the hip joint ?

A. No, it does not necessarily follow ; you very often see an abscess follow from any simple puncture.

Q. Might it come from a diseased bursa ?

A. I don't know of any bursa in that position.

Q. You think it could not have come from a diseased bursa ?

A. I don't think it could; I don't know of any bursa there, generally.

Q. Might it not have come from a healthy bursa, or diseased bursa, or abscess of a scrofulous character ?

A. Well, I have been answering your questions about abscess.

(Question repeated.)

A. I don't know of any bursa then at that point.

Q. You think it might have come ?

A. I don't know of any bursa there.

Q. From an abscess of a scrofulous character?

A. No.

Q. From a bursa in that neighbourhood, healthy or diseased?

A. I say at that point.

Q. I ask if it might have come from a healthy or diseased bursa?

A. I answer there is none there, as a general rule.

Q. Then it might have come from either?

A. No, I don't think so.

Q. If the joint had been injured in the operation, and this abscess, or what you observed there, were the result of that injury, would not the joint, when you examined it, have been all the way through involved, more or less?

A. Joints are opened without inflammation occurring sometimes, and again a small puncture in the joint is regarded as a very dangerous thing; at the same time there is history of doctors resorting to opening the hip joint in the early period of the disease : it is very bad practice, in my opinion.

Q. You don't think the hip was diseased?

A. There was no great indication when I saw it.

Q. Did you see the slightest indication of a diseased hip joint?

A. Yes, hectic fever; and a fluid oozing from it very much like synovial fluid was there, and so I suppose it was.

Q, Any other indication?

A. Well, the child was emaciated, and had all the signs of hectic fever—hot skin.

Q. Are there any other signs of hip disease than you have mentioned?

A. Yes, a great many.

Q. In what stage do you see the symptom?

A. Well, there is hectic fever in one stage, supposing the joint to be diseased, and there are symptoms allied to hip diseases—allied to those accompanying hip diseases.

Q. What?

A. Hectic fever—manifested by hotness of skin, quickness of pulse, emaciation, restlessness, want of appetite, and so forth.

Q. Would it not come from an abscess?

A. It depended on what kind of an abscess it was.

Q. Scrofulous abscess?

A. It depended on what kind of scrofulous abscess it was; no, it might not, because people go about the streets with them on their necks and without fever.

Q. Any hip disease without fever?

A. Yes.

Q. Do you remember the commencement of the action against Dr. Sayre?

A. I paid very little attention.

Q. Did you hear of it?

A. I dare say I did.

Q. Do you remember the child being subjected to inspection of physicians under order of the Court?

A. Yes.

Q. Do you remember that was on November 19, or in November, 1868?

A. I took no interest in the case, and do not now, nor the parties connected with it.

Q. Did you not tell Dr. Vaughan, on the examination, that Dr. Sayre had punctured the hip joint?

A. I thought at the time.

Q. Did you tell him so?

A. I dare say I did.

Q. Did you tell the mother?

A. I cannot say.

Q. You told Dr. Vaughan?

A. It is very likely, it had all the symptoms of it, and I could not account for the synovial coming in such quantities.

Q. Did he tell you of an abscess?

A. I do not think so.

Q. Did he say that an exploring needle had been used for abscess?

A. He told me there was a puncture made.

Q. If he had told you that a large quantity of matter had escaped, and continued to flow for five or six hours?

A. I think it would have come from the hip joint.

Q. You think it would have come from the hip joint ?

A. I thought so at the time.

Q. You don't say you examined the child in November, 1868 ?

A. I told you I am not perfect about dates.

Q. The seasons of the year you will be more apt to remember ; don't you know you examined the child in the spring only ?

A. I saw it once, but I cannot tell when I saw her ; I am very fond of making friends by cutting acquaintance.

Q. Well, if the hip was diseased, would both limbs be of the same length ?

A. They might be, or might not be.

Q. Well, ordinarily, would it be ?

A. It depends on what stage.

Q. In the stage which I have indicated by this large amount of matter ?

A The mere length does not alter much until some time after the disease has occurred ; the length may be varied by the synovial being thrown out : the disease does not shorten it for some time.

Q. Suppose she was lying down on the sofa on the 19th November, 1868, lying naturally, and that the limbs could be extended the full length without any tilting of the pelvis, and the two limbs were carefully measured and found to be of the same length, 20¾ inches, and the right limb could be flexed, and the left one could not be flexed so freely, and rotation, adduction, and abduction took place without paining her, what would you state as to hip joint disease ?

A. I don't think it was ; it don't look like hip disease ; usually hip diseases are accompanied by certain signs.

Q. Then from the signs indicated, you think that the disease did not exist ?

A. The question is so long ; I do not think so from such signs as you mentioned ; I don't think such symptoms as you mentioned, all taken together, would indicate the ordinary signs of hip disease.

Q. But would they not indicate—the signs which I have mentioned—the absence of hip disease ?

A. Not absolutely.

Q. Usually ?

A. Well, I say very commonly; those symptoms all exist most commonly.

Q. And yet hip disease ?

A. I have handled a child with a hip disease, and not made great complaint, and still the disease was going on.

Q. Does hip disease exist where the signs exist ?

A. Generally there are manifestations of pain; but all this business of length, &c., are not altogether associated with hip disease.

Q. Generally would not these signs indicate ?

A. You want me to say; you want me to get an idea that there is a different length in hip disease; it is not so always, it depends on the stage.

Q. What I want to ask is, that the signs which I have suggested do not indicate the absence of hip disease ?

A. Some do and some don't.

Q. Taking them altogether, do they not indicate the absence of hip disease ?

A. Ordinarily they do; I told you at first there were no great signs of hip disease.

Q. Suppose there were a concussion upon the left knee of the child, over the trochanter major, without any show of pain whatever, what would you say as to the existence of hip disease ?

A. There might or might not be; it is a very deceptive sign; you see fellows thump about the hip joint until they make it sore, and then it is said they have hip disease.

Q. Suppose the finger was pressed firmly upon the illiac fossa and no pain produced, what would that indicate, the absence or existence of hip disease ?

A. I don't think it would. What do you mean, outside or in ?

Q. Suppose there was no evidence of pain, would you say there was hip disease?

A. The illiac fossa has nothing to do with the hip disease; you cannot reach it with the finger; it is away from it.

Q. What is the shape and form of the limb, when there is hip disease?

A. I have to ask what stage.

Q. In the stage in which you saw the child?

A. It might assume any form, natural or unnatural.

Q. Did you see anything to indicate hip disease?

A. Yes; the hip was swollen, and there was a great disturbance about the hip joint?

Q. Could she walk?

A. I can't say; the child lay in bed; the child was so feeble that I did not get her out of that position; the child could not walk easily; the child was so weak she could not walk, on account of debility. I didn't think she would live.

Q. When did you see her?

A. I saw her within two or three weeks.

Q. Has the child got hip disease now?

A. I don't think it has.

Q. What was the matter?

A. The father brought the child—

Q. Did you examine it?

A. Not particularly.

Q. But you did examine the hip?

A. Not particularly; I saw the child move a little.

Q. You examined it, and are able now to express the opinion that it has not hip disease?

A. I did not say so.

Q. What do you say now?

A. The child has no signs of hip disease.

Q. How does it walk?

A. The child seems to be in the last stages now.

Q. From what cause, in your opinion?

A. I do not know.

Q. Now then—

WITNESS: There is one thing: it has been said that I volunteered to come.

Q. Who said so?

A. I heard it outside.

Mr. SHAFER: Don't listen to such a thing.

WITNESS: I heard this man, Sayre, say that it was Dr. Carnochan's case and Dr. Parker's; I was subpœnaed by the other side, I believe; I want to prevent that opinion being held in regard to coming here.

Q. Do I understand you to say that you are not able to state what the difficulty is?

A. I don't know about the child; I took no interest in the child's case at all.

Q. Did you ever make an examination to determine the matter?

A. The child was a scrofulous child.

Q. Would that be an adequate cause for the emaciated and feeble condition of the child.

A. I don't know—possibly.

Q. Does it look so—as if there was some latent disease about her?

A. The child is an unhealthy child, evidently.

Q. Was it an unhealthy child when you saw her?

A. Yes.

Q. Has it become more so since?

A. The child is better than when I saw her.

Q. It looks like a constitutional difficulty, does it not?

A. Yes, sir.

Redirect by Mr. James:

Q. Is it very easy to determine a discharge from an abscess and synovial fluid from an orifice?

A. Well, of course, an abscess means a collection of matter: the discharge of the synovial fluid is manifested by the discharge of the fluid that goes by that name.

Recross by Mr. Shafer :

Q. Is it not difficult to determine the difference after the lapse of four or five months after the abscess has been opened ?

A. If the abscess is an acute abscess or chronic abscess; a cold abscess is generally so purulent in matter, that there is no trouble.

Q. Is there a difference between serum and synovial fluid ?

A. There is an accepted difference.

Q. What is the difference ?

A. There is a different kind of membrane ; there is a serous membrane and a synovial membrane.

Q. Is it not difficult to determine the color ?

A. No, serous fluid is not so glairy or viscid.

Q. Is it not difficult to tell without a microscope ?

A. No, sir ; they knew what the synovial fluid was before the microscope was known.

Q. Suppose there is a sanious discharge from a chronic abscess, is there any difficulty ?

A. Sanious fluid is a fluid of half pus, and serous fluid mixed with blood.

Q. Tell us the chemical composition of synovial fluid ?

A. Synovial is made up of one thing and another, sometimes there are salts in it, epethelium in it, and there are various other things.

Q. Did you examine it with a microscope ?

A. I have looked at it when I was a boy ; any man that don't know the difference between them by sight or touch had better get out of the profession as soon as he can.

By Dr. Swinburne :

Q. They have asked the usual course an opened joint takes ; well, for instance, you have taken out the cartilage, what would be the natural course of that, provided that it goes on to resolution ?

A. The patient gets well without any pain, generally.

Q. Well, the question that next follows that : how long would synovial fluid continue to run from that joint?

A. It depends on the kind of wound that was made.

Q. How long would it run?

A. The synovial capsules will close up—

Q In what length of time, in your experience?

A. Well, we consider a case operated upon for an extraction of the cartilage of the knee joint ought to be healed in ten or twelve days.

Q. Suppose the reverse follows, and inflammation comes on, how long would you have pus secreted?

A. You might have pus for twenty-four or forty-eight hours : I should expect to see pus for four or five days.

Q. Suppose a person has a wound open for three months and synovial fluid is discharged?

A. It is not usual.

Q. After a scrofulous abscess has been opened, say three months, and it does not heal, what is your experience as to the character of the fluid?

A. It is different from the ostensible manifestations of synovial fluid ; it is sometimes more or less limpid, and it is not so tenacious or glairy ; it is more of the character of the white of an egg.

Q. Whether inflammation supervened or did not, as to the open joint, how long would you expect it to flow and the joint remain healthy, and no injury happen to the joint?

A. It should not flow long.

Q. How long?

A. For a week, ten days, or a fortnight.

By Mr. SHAFER to Dr. Parker :

Q. You remember the occasion or occasions when Dr. Vaughan called with the little girl at your house?

A. The first call I do, sir.

Q. Did you tell him then that what you saw was synovial fluid?

A. No, sir.

Q. But you did tell him that Dr. Sayre had punctured the hip joint?

A. No, sir.

Mr. Shafer to Mr. James: This is your case; have you other evidence?

Mr. James: No; I may want to put another question or two to Dr. Vaughan, but you need not stop for that.

Mr. Shafer: We have no objection to their doing that.

Mr. James: I would state to the Referees that I have received information that Dr. Swinburne is an intimate friend of Dr. Sayre's, and there was some case, I shall be able to verify it at the next meeting, in which Dr. Sayre performed some operation in which death resulted; I do not make any imputation, but I am told that Dr. Swinburne went, as a friend of Dr. Sayre, to compromise it; if Dr. Swinburne does stand in such relations to Dr. Sayre, he is not a proper gentleman to act as Referee in this case, and I believe that we shall show all these facts, from information brought to me; I mention it in Dr. Swinburne's presence; I apprehend that Dr. Swinburne will be guided by the same motives that the gentleman before was influenced by, if he has any friendship or intimacy of any kind. I put it to him, that he should not preside here.

Judge McKean: To my own personal knowledge, I say, that when in Court, before a Judge and the Jury that was empannelled, it was proposed by the counsel for the plaintiff, to refer this case: at first we objected to it—we refused, but the other side pressed the matter, and several names were mentioned; to my own personal knowledge, Dr. Sayre did not mention the name of Dr. Swinburne, and when his name was suggested by, I think, Mr. Shafer, Dr. Sayre said at first: "No, he is politically very hostile to me;" but, said Mr. Shafer, "don't let politics have anything to do with it;" then, said Dr. Sayre, "I won't object to anybody; refer it if you choose; take anybody;"

and without any procurement of Dr. Sayre, and upon the ready assent of counsel, Dr. Swinburne was selected.

Mr. SHAFER: Let me add to that; it is as painful a thing, entirely ignorant as I am of the matter, as I ever knew, and, intimate as Dr. Swinburne and myself are as old friends, it is very painful that the matter should have assumed this shape; but whatever may be said on the other side by affidavit, innuendo or otherwise, he will be able to show that he is a proper person to sit, for his delicacy and high honor would not have permitted him to sit for a moment if he felt incompetent to do so; when the other side suggested a reference, Mr. Gage and Judge McKean were opposed to it very bitterly, and Dr. Sayre also; I favored it, and upon the reference being made he wished that we should have first-class men; then I mentioned several names to the counsel, after which I went to Dr. Sayre and told him the names which were assented to by the opposing counsel; he said, "No, that won't do; Swinburne is politically "hostile to me;" I said, "Don't let politics interfere; take a "man of intelligence;" "Well," said Dr. Sayre, "take any-"body, but I would rather have three doctors," and then Dr. Sayre, in answer to a suggestion made by Mr. James that Dr. Parker and Dr. Carnochan should be referees, said, "Yes, take "anybody."

Mr. JAMES: No, I never suggested it; it would be absurd to name my own witnesses.

Mr. SHAFER: Oh yes, you did.

Dr. SWINBURNE: If this matter is painful to others, it is very painful to me; I have spent seven years here, and I think I have been to Dr. Sayre's house twice a year, and went there simply in reference to surgery; Dr. Carnochan has been always my friend, and has been associated with me in the Board of Health for three or four years; it is true that Dr. Sayre was with Mayor Gunther when I first came to the city: but our relations were the same as any other surgeons.

Mr. Shafer: Well, what about this case that you compromised

Dr. Swinburne: There is no case of that kind ; there was a case of a child that came down from Albany and had an operation performed and the case proved fatal, and the family made a good deal of fuss about it; Dr. Sayre asked me if I knew the family, and told me the history of the case ; I never saw Dr. Sayre in reference to it; I spoke to the clergyman connected with the diocese; I said, here is a case of Dr. Sayre's that is, perhaps, going to make the Doctor trouble, and that was all there was of it; that is all I know of the case.

Mr. James to one of the Counsel: I don't want to examine

Dr. Swinburne: Examine as much as you see fit.

Mr. Shafer: Well, if there is anything of this character, let the gentleman make his motion in the ordinary way, and let us meet it; but I must say that I never before, in my life, heard a gentleman—

Dr. Swinburne: I felt as if I wanted to understand this case. I wished to give them all the chance they wanted to prove their case, and so said to Mr. Traphagen, when they considered about eliminating some of the testimony of Dr. Parker—

Mr. Traphagen: Yes, he said that they ought to be allowed to put it in, and we have allowed it for that reason.

Mr. Shafer: This matter is all foreign and unwarranted.

Mr. Traphagen: We cannot take cognisance of this here. That must be determined elsewhere.

Dr. Swinburne: Perhaps, for a year before coming here, I formed Dr. Sayre's acquaintance, and I never knew him before. Both of us were interested in surgery, so are Dr. Wood and

Dr. Carnochan, and all these gentlemen, and the same relation
I bear towards Dr. Sayre I bear towards them. When I and
another were candidates for the position of Health Officer,
before I was appointed, Dr. Carnochan said that he would
rather see me there than the other candidate.

Mr Jamies: I have said nothing about socially. I state, in
the discharge of my duty, I took the responsibility of saying
that there was a patient whose case ended fatally. As you
yourself expressed it, there was likely to be some trouble, and that
I am told Dr. Sayre was the operator.

Dr. Swinburne: You used the word agent, or suggested as
much.

Mr. James: I did not; I will stand by my words.

Judge McKean: In reference to this it would seem that this
eminent surgeon, Dr. Sayre, has lost one patient.

Mr. James: It may be as well to enter my protest against
Dr. Swinburne, making it the subject of a motion to the Court.

Mr. Traphagen: We have no objection to a protest being
entered.

Mr. James: Then I wish to insert on the record that I enter
a protest.

Plaintiff rests.

Judge McKean, opening for the defence, said: May it please
the gentlemen of the reference, it seems now to be the theory of
the plaintiff's counsel that the little girl in question was taken
to the defendant, Dr. Sayre, not for an operation, but for examination; not for practice, but for an opinion; and the mother of
the little girl, upon her direct examination, sought to convey to
the Referees that impression. I purpose to read one paragraph

from the complaint. After stating certain other matters, the plaintiff proceeds thus :

" IV That the plaintiff, on or about the 10th of March, 1868, " was taken by her mother to the defendant, he being a surgeon " as aforesaid, to be treated by him for a swelling and an injury " in the neighborhood of one of her hips, and the cause of " which injury was not known to the mother of the plaintiff, " and the defendant in his capacity of such surgeon was then " consulted by and on behalf of the plaintiff, and was employed " and then undertook such employment as surgeon to heal and " cure the plaintiff."

I take it, gentlemen, that this allegation in the complaint which has brought us into Court, disposes of that question ; but you may remember that, while upon her direct examination, the mother sought to have it understood that the defendant's opinion only was sought, yet, upon her cross-examination, she did admit, after I pressed her somewhat, that it was for treatment as well as examination that the girl was taken to Dr. Sayre. The mother's testimony, gentlemen, not only does not show that there was any rashness, or haste, or roughness, or want of care, on the part of Dr. Sayre, but it clearly shows that he used the utmost care ; made a careful, and, as the result showed, a skillful examination of the little girl, and then proceeded to the operation. The only thing upon which she lays stress is this, making no pretence that he used any rudeness, harshness, or haste, nor that he plunged an instrument, as she said in her conversation with Dr. Parker, but did not say in her testimony, that he plunged an instrument into this swelling ; but the only thing upon which she seems to lay stress is that Dr. Sayre cut her little girl. Well, now, we can well understand how a kind-hearted, sensitive mother, who is fond of her little girl, illiterate, ill-informed, with all the excitability of her race—the Irish race—should view that matter. She went with the intention of having it done, but when the cutting came to be done she was horrified at the idea. She seems, poor woman, in her excitement, in her affection for the little girl, and in her want of information, she seems to be thoroughly ignorant of the fact, that it is the business of the surgeon to cut. She seems to be entirely unconscious of the fact that the surgeon, when he sees death approaching slowly upon its victim, makes it his business to fight death with a knife. The Doctor sees the condition of the little girl, and after making what the proof has shown to have been a most skillful diagnosis of the case, he steps in between the fell destroyer and the little girl, draws his knife, and says "Halt!"—and the mother is terrified. That is all that the mother's testimony amounts to—that Dr. Sayre cut the little girl.

Vaughan, by courtesy called "Dr. Vaughan," a druggist's clerk, who will not tell what medical institution he has attended, for the very good reason that he has not attended any; who will not tell where he got his diploma, for the very good reason that he has none; who cannot tell the difference between synovial, serous, and sanious fluids; who cannot name any one of the ligaments of the hip joint; who, after being pressed, has either the frankness, or, with the hope of being let up, has the shrewdness to say that he is not an expert, but that he takes his patients to those who are skillful, and who are experts. This man Vaughan is called in here as an expert, and is the physician of the plaintiff's family; now, gentlemen, I will not, at present, take up any more valuable time by commenting on the testimony of such a man.

As for Mr. Walsh, I shall spend no time on his testimony, for the reason that all he relates is hearsay, and the witnesses whose statements he relates as hearsay have been themselves called, and I shall, therefore, spend no time on him.

Dr. Willard Parker, an eminent surgeon of this city, is called; he saw the child on the last of May, or the first of June, 1868, some two months after the operation. There was then no hip disease. He says he found a liquid behind the hip joint on the buttock. The mother sought to make it appear that Dr. Sayre had plunged a needle, I believe she called it, several times into that region—but mind, the mother, in her testimony, used no such language, neither upon the direct nor upon the cross-examination—but in her excited way, talking to Dr. Parker, she used expressions that she would not use when she was testifying. "That fluid," Dr. Parker said, "was glairy and viscid; that is "all I know about it; whether it was synovial fluid or not I "cannot determine." When questioned by the plaintiff's counsel, this question was put: "Can you give any opinion as to what "it was?" Answer: "No, sir; I cannot very definitely." Q. "To the best of your knowledge, was that synovial fluid?" Answer: "From all knowledge, I suspected it to be synovial "fluid." Question: "To a gentleman of your experience, is "the synovial fluid detectable?" Answer: "I think not; not "absolutely from other kinds of fluid; we have what are called "'bursal sacs,' where you have the same." Q. "Would not "you have it sometimes from an old abscess?" A. "It is impos- "sible absolutely, by any means, to determine one from the "other; but taking the several kinds by a microscopic examina- "tion and chemical analysis, there would be shades of difference "discovered; but nothing of that kind was done by me."

Now, I will spend a little time, but I shall not spend much, upon the testimony already in, in order that we may inquire how the case now stands at this stage of its progress. Dr. Parker proceeds to say, that "subsequent effects would be "serious in the shape of inflammation of the joint, if the "synovial fluid was let out. Two months would have been "likely to have produced active inflammation in the joint, "unless the discharge closed up." But, mind you, the discharge was not closed up, and yet there was no disease of the hip. Speaking of the discharge, and whether it was synovial fluid or not, Dr. Parker says: "I simply say that I could not "give, or would not give, it as a positive opinion at all." He has seen the child several times since, saw her the last of August, or fore part of September, and he says: "I found a "condition of things which confirmed my previous opinion, that "the hip joint was not diseased. The child became very sick "indeed after that—very. When inflammation supervenes on "the membrane lining of the cavity, it produces very serious

" results indeed, in the shape of destruction of the joint, and dis-
" placement of the head of the bone, and a variety of that kind of
" thing. I saw the child about six months ago, about January
" —no difficulty about the hip joint at all. She had extensive
" abscesses occurring about the body."

Now, taking the statement of Dr. Parker, that serious results
would be apt to supervene in the short space of two months, if
the orifice was not closed up and the discharge ceased—taking
that in connection with the fact that he saw her six months ago,
and there were numerous abscesses on the body, and that there
was no disease of the hip joint, which must have been the
result if the synovial fluid had been let out, and the joint
punctured two years ago—the conclusion is irresistible that the
hip joint was not punctured, and that the synovial fluid was not
let out. He goes on to say, that there was no shortening of
the limb, no contraction, no abduction, no adduction of the
limb, and no evidence of a disease hip.

Q. "Could she walk?" was asked, "at that time, six months
ago?"

A. "I think she could, very well."

Dr. Carnochan has been called, and while he differs from Dr.
Parker in some particulars, yet the whole substance of his testimony amounts to this, taking it altogether, upon the direct and
cross-examination, that if there was such a discharge as the
counsel supposed, in putting his questions to him, and as has
been proved by the mother of the child, that that would not indicate any disease of the hip, and such a discharge could not be
of synovial fluid, and that when he saw her a few weeks ago in
Court, I think he said, there was no evidence of hip disease,
and that she was much better than when he had seen her on
the previous occasion, and that the case which the counsel supposed in putting his questions, would indicate an abscess rather
than a diseased hip joint

Now, gentlemen, if there has been any malpractice, or any
injury resulting from negligence to this little girl, the onus of
the proof of that injury lies on the other side. Who, by the

proof, was guilty of negligence and malpractice ? It is admitted by the mother of the child that when she excitedly seized her child to take it away, that she was directed by Dr. Sayre to bring the child back again in two or three days, and that she never did bring the child back ; that he was never allowed thereafter to see the child to prescribe for it, and was never consulted in regard to it. And it would seem that the learned physicians and surgeons to whom the child was taken could hardly be excused for relying simply upon the statement of the illiterate and excited mother and the very ignorant "Dr. Vaughan." And yet these learned physicians, who are called by the other side, and whose testimony in the main operates in favor of my client, these learned physicians and surgeons themselves admit that they did not probe this abscess or swelling, whatever it might be, on or near the hip of the little girl ; that they did not know nor learn, from either "Dr. Vaughan" or the mother, that there had been an abscess there and that pus had been let out of it. But the most that they seemed to have learned was from the mother, who, in her excited condition, was induced to say that the doctor took what she called a needle and plunged it into that region. And it would seem as if these learned physicians and surgeons had taken this statement and that of the ignorant "Dr. Vaughan," and so far as they gave any directions in regard to the treatment of the little girl, predicated their opinions and their prescriptions upon the statements of these two persons.

Now, gentlemen, without setting myself up to judge in these medical and surgical matters, it has occurred to me that these medical gentlemen ought to have done somewhat as Dr. Sayre did, make a most thorough examination themselves, and perhaps an exploration of this cold abscess, or whatever it might be, and from what they discovered then, rather than from what they were told by these two persons, reach their conclusions and make their prescriptions. But, notwithstanding this seeming negligence on the part of the plaintiff's parents and guardians in failing to take back to Dr. Sayre, and possibly some degree of haste and want of attention on the part of the learned gentlemen to whom the child was afterwards taken—it would seem that, notwithstanding these things, the child is in a better condition of health now than she was some two years ago

I agree with the learned counsel who opened the case for the plaintiff, that eminent men in the profession may often make mistakes. If they might not, if they could not, then it would simply be to say that eminent men are perfect men. But if any mistakes have been made by eminent men in anything touching this case, it seems to me that they are the eminent men upon whom the learned counsel, to some extent, has relied, and not the eminent gentleman who performed this operation, and whom I have the honor to defend.

The history of the case is about this, gentlemen : This little girl was brought by her mother, by direction of " Dr Vaughan," to Dr. Sayre's office, but was first examined by Dr. Paine, who was Dr. Sayre's assistant—a very skillful physician and surgeon. He, after making his own diagnosis of the case, took the precaution to take the child up stairs, that Dr. Sayre might also examine her, and, if necessary, perform an operation upon her. It so happened that there were several other medical gentlemen— three or four, I believe—of eminence, in their profession, in the office with Dr. Sayre at the time. The little girl was stripped and carefully examined, not merely for the purposes of an opinion, but for an operation, if the Doctor, after examination, should deem it necessary.

Now, gentlemen, in law, Dr. Sayre was required only to exercise ordinary care and skill—that was all, but you shall be convinced, if you are not already convinced, that in this case he exercised extraordinary care and skill. He made a careful examination of the swelling, and the Doctor differed in opinion in regard to its character from some of the learned gentlemen who were present with him. They discussed it. It was thought by some of the learned gentlemen that it was a tumor, and that it should not be opened. It was the opinion of this client of ours, who, as I have already said, was required to exercise only ordinary care and skill in his profession—it was the opinion of this man of extraordinary skill, and who, on this occasion, examined the case with extraordinary care, that it was an abscess. He took his exploring needle, which I need not explain to medical gentlemen, and very likely not to legal gentlemen, though, if these legal gentlemen were as ignorant of it as myself when I came into this case, it might be as well to say that it is a very slender instrument, a little larger than a large sized needle, in a scabbard. The point of this needle (the instrument being taken up by the counsel), passed through the top of the scabbard, and with that instrument, or such an instrument, the Doctor explored and examined the swelling, and put the needle carefully in and then drew out the blade, leaving the hollow scabbard in, to see if any pus would come out of the tube. Some of the gentlemen, at first, who saw no pus, said : " Doctor, you will have to give it up; it is not an abscess." " Wait," said the Doctor ; the scabbard fell down, showing it was in a hollow place. They watched it a moment, and a drop or two of pus came out; then the Doctor took the histoury and cut the opening, and the confined pus burst out on the floor. Then Dr. Paine got the basin (one exhibited), and held it to the opening, and caught it nearly full of the matter, which the mother explained to you in her own language. During all this time the little girl seemed not to be hurt at all ; she made no outcry, and I believe it relieved her, for the confined pus gave her an uneasy feeling ; at all events, the mother was, in her excitement, going to carry off the girl, but Dr. Sayre told her not to do so, that he had not done with her, that he had not dressed it. He then dressed the swelling, cleaned it off, and poured in some preparation, which caused some smarting, and then the little girl made an outcry. Then the mother became excited, extremely excited, and she caught the child up and went off in the excited manner which she admitted, Dr. Sayre saying : "Bring that child back in the course of two or three days."

Now, gentlemen, this is the case, and not only is it not a case of malpractice, but a case of very extraordinary care and skill, and the operation resulted beneficially to the little girl, though it is possible, from the fact that she is a scrofulous subject, that

she has not fully recovered from the latent disease in her system.
We shall, without moving to dismiss the complaint at this stage,
call a few medical gentlemen, in order that you may know all
about this case. When the evidence is all in, we shall ask you
to make such a report as justice and law shall seem to require.

Dr. Paine called and sworn for defendant. Examined by
Judge McKean :

Q. You are a physician and a surgeon ?

A. I am.

Q. How long have you been so ?

A. Ever since the year 1862

Q. Where did you study ?

A. Buffalo University and Long Island College, Brooklyn.

Q. You graduated in that year ?

A. No, sir ; in the winter of 1863-64 ; I was in the army as
Assistant-Surgeon before I graduated.

Q. In the late war ?

A. Yes, sir.

Q. How long did you serve there ?

A. I went in 1862 ; came back in 1863 ; graduated in the
winter of 1863-64, and went back again until the close of the
war.

Q. There you saw a good deal of practice ?

A. I was Assistant-Surgeon of Surgeon-in-Chief and Brigade
Surgeon

Q. Since the war you have been practicing in this city ?

A. Yes, sir.

Q. Were you in the spring of 1863 assisting Dr. Sayre ?

A. Yes, sir.

Q. Do you remember the little girl, the plaintiff ?

A. Very well.

Q. About what time was that ?

A. In the spring of 1868, either in March or April ; I don't
remember which month.

Q. Brought to you first ?

A. Yes, sir ; she was not brought to me, she was brought to Dr. Sayre, but it was my business to examine her.

Q. You saw her first ?

A. Yes, sir; in the lower office.

Q. In the same building ?

A. Yes, sir.

Q. You examined her ?

A. I did.

Q. What did you find ?

A. I found a swelling reaching from the sacro illiac junction and which came down here (illustrating by the model of the pelvis), and stuck out here, the other hip being of its natural size.

Q. That hip was considerably larger ?

A. Yes, sir.

Q. The mother of the child was with it ?

A. Yes, sir.

Q. How did it resemble this ? (Showing the casting).

A. Very much, but not quite in that position.

Q. You did not explore it in the office ?

A. No, sir ; I examined it for some ten minutes, because I considered it an interesting case.

Q. Whom did you find with Dr. Sayre ?

A. Dr. Neftel, of this city, Dr. Gross, Jr., of Philadelphia.

Q. Well, you submitted the case to the Doctor ?

A. Yes, sir.

Q. What did he do ?

A. He made his own diagnosis in regard to it, and then he said, " Gentlemen, this is an abscess, and to prove it to you, I " will introduce an exploring needle, and you will see that " matter will follow."

Q. This was done after the examination by the Doctors ?

A. Yes, sir ; and quite a long examination, because we had some talk as regards the nature of the swelling, whether it was a tumor or an abscess ; he then introduced an exploring needle, and after pulling it out pus came from the canula, and then, to make it more clear, he introduced the knife about an inch and a half above the hip joint.

Q. Introduced a needle?

A. Yes, sir; and then after pulling it out—the needle—he introduced a bistoury in the same puncture, and then, I did not measure the amount, but I should say that a pint or a pint and a half of what Dr. Gross calls scrofulous matter followed the knife.

Q. Describe the manner of its coming out.

A. It gushed out in a stream two feet from the child and struck the floor.

Q. Came out in a spurt?

A. Yes, sir; came out in this basin; he used to use this basin for washing out the ear, but nothing else was handy, and it spirted over this.

Q. Half-a-pint or so was there?

A. Yes, sir; I should think from a pint to a pint and a-half of matter altogether.

Q. And that was not at hand at first?

A. No, sir; I got that to catch the matter.

Q. Explain again the kind of matter?

A. There is a great difference in pus; there is what is called laudable pus, and there are other kinds of pus; this matter was no more like synovial fluid than cold water, not a bit more; it was simple pus, nothing else, it came from a cold abscess.

Q. Did you notice when the exploring needle was entered, the angle at which it entered?

A. I do not remember in regard to that, although I was close to the Doctor; I do not remember it more than passing an exploring needle into any other abscess; I believe it was carried greatly backwards.

Q. Away from the hip joint?

A. Away from it.

Q. How was the child lying?

A. On the sofa.

Q. On her face?

A. I think so, either on the face or side.

Q. What then was done after the pus was let out ?

A. Dr. Sayre took a solution which he had there, a mixture of carbolic acid and linseed oil, and put it on cloth and put a bandage on, and he said to the woman, I want you to come back in one or two days; he said to me " I want you to attend to. it," and also to another in the office, by the name of Belden, " I want you to go down and see the child; " but as he had told her to come back. neither of us went there.

Q. What did she say at the time ?

A. I don't remember, she was very much excited at the time, crying, &c.

Q. When she brought the child to you, or when she brought it to Dr. Sayre, what did she want done ?

A. I don't remember ; I suppose she wanted the child cured, but I don't remember what she said.

Q. There are a great number of patients every day ?

A. A great number ; yes, sir.

Q. Did she object to any operation being performed ?

A. I can't say as regards that.

Q. She got excited after it was performed ?

A. Yes, sir.

Q. When did the mother manifest the most excitement and make the most objection ?

A. After it was operated upon the child commenced crying, of course, and the mother flew at it, caught it up, and ran from the office ; I expected her to be back.

Q. What was this pus ?

A. This is such as comes from cold abscesses.

Q. Describe it generally ?

A. After pus of this kind has been taken out, it remains in two portions, one portion being oily, and the other contains shreds or debris of the structure in which it is contained, also grumous blood; in fact different from laudable pus, that merely containing pus globules in pus liquor; this was real pus, and pus of the worst form—scrofulous pus ; I think if kept for two hours it would have smelt very bad indeed ; if I mistake not, I then thought there was a sort of chesnut odor about it ; .I looked at the pus very carefully, because I was interested in the case.

Q. Did you think, and if so what, in regard to its being surprising that she did not return ?

A. I believe I asked the Doctor if she had been back and the Doctor asked if she was not back ; I expected her, that I might dress the wound.

Q. He has several to assist him ?

A. Yes, sir ; he has one assistant always, and several students to assist him.

Q. Are you there now ?

A. I am not; no, sir.

Q. Do you know of his having a great many hip diseases to attend to ?

A. Probably more than any man in the United States.

Q. And many pauper cases, has he not ?

A. A great many.

Q. What was this understood to be when it came ?

A. I know Dr. Sayre never got anything for it ; I suppose he looked upon it as a charitable case ; he never asked for any fee ; in fact, I don't think he knew the woman's name.

Q. Did you notice any difference between the care and skill which he exercised in regard to patients, whether pauper or not ?

A. He treats his pauper patients, sometimes, better than the other patients.

Q. Is he not in the habit of keeping a record of his interesting cases ?

A. Yes, sir.

Q. And that, too, irrespective of the question, whether he is paid or not ?

A. Yes, sir ; certainly ; in fact I know Mrs. Walsh never paid him anything at that time.

Q. Was anything said about that at the time ?

A. Not the slightest word.

Q. The Doctor is in the habit of having photographs taken of his interesting patients?

A. Yes, sir; he sends them to a photographer.

By Mr. SHAFER:

Q. I understood you to answer that there was no hip disease?

A. I did not find any at the time.

Q. And this exploring needle did not go anywhere near the hip joint?

A. No, no, no.

Q. How far from the hip joint?

A. Three or four inches.

Q. You state that from actual observation?

A. I was there and saw the operation performed.

Q. You state that as a fact?

A. Yes, sir.

Q. It could not have been nearer than three or four inches?

A. No, sir.

Q. What was the depth from the outer portion of the tumor you have mentioned, to the hip joint, as existing in this child, to send the needle, to strike the hip joint?

A. Six or seven inches.

Q. How far did it actually enter?

A. An inch or inch and a half; here is the puffy swelling (illustrating by model), and it had to go through there before it reached the hip joint; it had to travel forward and downward before striking the hip joint.

Mr. CROAK said he would wait before cross-examining witness, until Mr. James came.

Dr. NEFTEL called and sworn. Examined by Judge McKEAN:

Q. You are a physician and surgeon practising here?

A. Yes, sir.

Q. How long have you practised ?

A. Since 1852.

Q. In this city ?

A. No, St. Petersburgh, Russia ; I am a Russian myself.

Q. Were you in Dr. Sayre's office when an operation was performed on a little girl called Walsh ?

A. Yes ; I remember it was soon after my arrival here from Europe; I happened to be there and I saw the child brought by her mother, and examined by Dr. Sayre ; there was present also Dr. Gross of Philadelphia.

Q. How came you to go to the office ?

A. I went there because he had several very interesting surgical cases to show me, and I heard so much of him as a surgeon.

Q. And you carried a letter of introduction from Dr. Sims ?

A. From Dr. Sims, of London ; he was in Paris at that time ; I recollect what was a swelling, and Dr. Sayre examined it and found fluctuation, and he inserted an exploring needle and pus came out ; I am perfectly sure that he did not enter the joint or touch any bone ; that I am positive of.

Q. Then after entering the exploring needle he took the bistoury, did he not ?

A. I don't recollect ; I don't believe, but I am positive he did not enter the joint or touch any bone.

Q. You made an examination and stood by to assist ?

A. Yes, sir ; but I don't recollect ; I don't know whether he did anything else or not.

Q. You saw the exploration ?

A. Yes ; how he inserted the needle, and how the pus came out.

Q. Will you explain to the Referees where the swelling was ?

A. I confess I am not positive ; it was in the vicinity of the gluteal muscles ; as near as I can say, it was on the lower back of the dorsal region.

Q. Do you know how the little girl was lying ?

A. I think she was lying down.

Q. What was the character of the discharge that came out of it?

A. I cannot say without a microscopical examination ; it was pus, but I have not made a microscopical examination of it, and there may be something besides.

Q. Was there a large quantity ?

A. I think there was a large quantity, but I don't recollect.

Q. Do you remember his assistant taking a basin and catching it.

A. I think so, but I have forgotten the particulars.

Q. What was the character of the swelling ?

A. He introduced an exploring needle to find out what the matter was ; it was pus ; but where it came from we could not decide.

Q. You confined your attention to the swelling ?

A. To the swelling for the time being ; I think some one said it was not pus, but a tumor, but I am not sure ; but I recollect he introduced the exploratory needle, and the pus came out.

Q. From the fact that you found fluctuation, and found pus, what would you call the swelling — an abscess or tumor ?

A. It is called an abscess ; you may call it what you wish.

Q. What did he do in the way of dressing ?

A. I cannot say ; I have forgotten those particulars ; the only point of interest was, whether it was pus or not; Dr. Sayre said it was pus, and found it.

Q. You recollect the instrument being put in, and the result of it ?

A. I did not pay any attention to it, as the matter was of no interest.

Q. You have performed many surgical operations yourself?

A. Yes, sir ; a great many in Russia ; I was connected with the largest Imperial Hospital, and made a great many surgical operations; in fact, the begining of my professional career was a surgical one.

In answer to a question put by one of the counsel, Mr. Croak thought Mr. James had gone home.

Mr. TRAPHAGEN : It is not proper that counsel should leave the case in this manner.

Mr. ESTES : I do not see why he goes away.

Mr. SHAFER : He desires to have some action taken here that would act as a default. I am determined that we shall have nothing of this kind. His treatment of the reference has been most discourteous and most unusual ; there is nothing like it in the practice of this country, and yet I am so anxious that he shall not have a default, I shall ask Dr. Sayre to bring these witnesses here again, although it is a great inconvenience. I am satisfied that from the temper and trouble here to-day, and every day, if possible, he is going to subject Dr. Sayre to some litigation hereafter. If we are wrong we want it decided against us, and if right that it should be decided for us, and so I ask the Referees to hold the matter open.

By Mr. TRAPHAGEN :

Q. I should like to ask Dr. Neftel whether that was synovial fluid or not ?

A. It looked pus.

Q. Had it the resemblance of synovial fluid ?

A. Not at all.

Dr. SAYRE sworn.   Examined by Judge McKEAN :

Q. How long have you been a physician and surgeon ?

A. Since 1842.

Q. How long have you practised in this city ?

A. Since 1842.

Q. You remember the case of the little girl, Margaret Walsh, being brought to you, Doctor ?

A. Yes, sir ; very well.

Q. You remember Dr. Paine and the mother coming in ?

A. Very distinctly.

Q. Who were there ?

A. Dr. Neftel had come with a letter of introduction from Dr. Sims, Dr. Gross was there, Dr. Paine, who brought the child up, Dr. Belden, who is now in California in the army, Dr. Phillips of Washington, and Dr. Conover of New Jersey, who is now down in Washington; there might have been others there, but I remember those gentlemen very distinctly.

Q. Who introduced the case to you ?

A. Dr. Paine brought the child up ; he said it was an interesting case, and wanted me to look at it; he wanted a diagnosis; I then found the tumor on the left hip; the question was whether it was a fatty tumor or not (taking the plaster model) ; here was a case sent to me as a fatty tumor, and it was sent to be cut out, but upon examination I found it to be an abscess, and this child's case was very similar; this I refused to cut out, and was laughed at, at the time a good deal : the Doctors believed it to be a tumor; but I took this case and found it to be an abscess connected with the lung; I opened it, explored it, and discharged two pints of matter, and found that coughing blew a candle out placed at the opened abscess.

Mr. SHAFER here requested that the casting be allowed in evidence.

(Allowed.)

WITNESS continuing : And so you may have a pus at an immense distance from the region, that causes the pus ; Dr. Paine, my assistant, treats the poor patients, and when there is any extraordinary instance he brings it upstairs, and the reason he brought this up, was because it was so much like this (the plaster model) ; well, there was a discussion as to whether it was a fatty tumor or not; I asked Dr. Paine to bring me an exploring needle—this is the very needle used—and I went over the central part of the tumor in that manner (referring to model), passed it in and then pulled the needle out; for a moment nothing appeared, but the needle fell over (if it had stuck in anything solid it would have remained straight), and then matter dropped out of it; I then pulled it out and took a bistoury, and increasing the hole about half an inch, the matter spurted out two or three feet over the floor, and then Dr. Paine caught the balance of it; the child was perfectly quiet; the pain was not known to her; she was lying on her belly; I then called for Dr. Paine to get me the carbolic acid, and I opened the hole and poured it into it; this acid burned the child—it smarted, I presume; up to that time the mother was walking up and down the room, and did not even look at me when doing it; but as soon as I put the acid into the child, the mother acted like a crazy woman; she said "whirra—whirra—whirra," and said "do not operate upon the child," and I said "I am not going to operate upon the child"; it had already been done; after she left I told Dr. Paine to find out who the woman was; she said she would bring the child back the next day; I told Paine and the student to look after her, that I had opened an abscess, but the source of the abscess I did not know; the matter might come from a distant source, it might come from the spine, sacrum, or illium; this woman did not give me a chance to find the source, but ran away, and that was the last I saw of the child until it was in Court.

Q. What was the character of the pus?

A. It was pus and serum, and floculi of broken-down cellular tissue, some as big as the thumb; I made a hole three-quarters of an inch long, and I had to take the forceps to pull them out, and then the matter would run again; there were half a dozen thickened lumps, and with the lumps of cellular tissue in the basin and the pus, it was nearly half full, besides that upon the floor.

Q. What resemblance did it have to synovial fluid?

A. None at all; none at all; no more than my fist resembles that pelvis.

Q. And some time after that there would be, probably, a discharge of what character?

A. There would be a thin, glairy discharge, that would probably resemble synovial fluid, at the first appearance of it.

Q. And by the touch?

A. Yes, sir.

Q. Could you tell such a discharge as you are now describing from synovial fluid ?

A. They don't look alike.

Q. I am speaking of subsequent days or weeks ?

A. Probably.

Q. In respect to the discharge from such an abscess, could you tell such a discharge from synovial fluid without microscopical and chemical examination ?

A. No, sir.

Q. In what direction did you put that instrument ?

A. Well, suppose that tumor there (referring to the model) to be brought half an inch lower, you would get a counterpart of the thing; it was about three inches from the top of the trochanter major, and half way down between that and the posterior crest of the illium; I put it in about an inch or an inch and a half; I didn't get within three inches of the bone.

Q. Was there any disease of the hip joint ?

A None at all.

Q. Did you examine her?

A. Yes; perfectly—carefully.

Q. What did you find ?

A. The joint perfectly normal and natural.

Q. The same length ?

A. Yes, and the joints perfectly complete.

Q. Would not a common boil make it tender ?

A. Oh, yes; make the muscles sore.

Q. I did not ask you the precise date ?

A. The 2d day of April, 1868 ?

By Mr. Traphagen :

Q. Is there any difference in the time ?

A. It has been said to be the 10th of March, but I can prove it by the servant man, who keeps a record of every one coming into the office, of every man, poor or rich, the day they come, and every morning I take off those able to pay, and the others I let go ; this woman was not brought on my book at all; the first I heard of the child afterwards was when I was sued sometime in the Fall; it was early in the Fall; I don't remember the date.

By Judge McKEAN :

Q. What pay did you get for this?

A. Nothing.

Q. You have had many cases of hip disease, have you not?

A. Yes, sir.

Q. How many in the course of a year?

A. I had three new cases to-day; one was from Wisconsin, one from Chicago, and one from New Orleans; there would be two or three a day.

Q. Many thousands in all?

A. No, sir.

Q. Many hundreds?

A. Yes, sir.

Q. You did not think it was possible that you touched the hip joint?

A. I know I could not; there is no possibility about it.

Mr. CROAK : It is understood that Mr. James has the privilege of cross-examining.

By Judge McKEAN :

Q. How far was it from the joint?

A. Even if the tumor had been over the joint it would have been four inches.

By Mr. TRAPHAGEN :

Q. At the time of this examination, did you think the hip was diseased?

A. No; I knew it was not diseased.

Q. Was it the impression of your associate?

A. No; to tell the truth, I took the child and took all the the clothes off, and then laid it down on the floor to have a solid place ; there is not a surgeon whose opinion is worth that (snapping his fingers), who would make an examination upon a bed to diagnosticate hip disease ; the peculiar deformity that takes place in the disease is absolutely and positively unmistakable.

By Mr. SHAFER :

Q. Was there any person there who said it was hip disease ?
A. The woman thought so.

By Dr. SWINBURNE :

Q. Any medical man ?
A. No, sir ; Dr. Paine discovered it to be a tumor, and the question came, whether it was fatty ; Dr. Neftel, as soon as he saw the fluid come out, said, "that satisfies me," but Dr. Gross and the others interested themselves about the matter, and I opened it ; I am satisfied that it was not hip joint disease ; I laid the child on the floor, and found I could bring the limb down to the ground without any tilting of the pelvis ; the joint cannot set straight if there is any fluid in it ; the fact of it is, the symptoms cannot be mistaken for anything else.

Q. You found the limbs all right ?
A. I found no evidence of disease in that hip joint at all ; it was examined for that purpose, and all that was found was that abscess, and as to the source of the abscess, I intended to get all the matter out of it, and find out where it came from, and if I had found out where it came from, I would have reached the root, and so cured the child, if possible.

By Mr. SHAFER :

Q. You were present at the examination made by Drs. Van Buren, Krackowizer and Hamilton ?
A. Yes, sir.
Q. And you found the hip joint all right ?
A. Perfect.
Q. You examined it with them ?

A. Yes, sir; the child can be brought now and examined by all the Doctors in the world, and she will be found in the same way now.

Judge McKEAN to Mr. Croak: You don't want to examine him now?

Mr. CROAK: I want to have the privilege hereafter.

By Mr. SHAFER to Dr. NEFTEL:

Q. What was the day you arrived from Europe?
A. The last day of March, 1868; and I recollect very well that I had not been to see him about a week.
Q. So that you were there the first days of April?
A. I was there about the first days of April.

Adjourned till next day, June 8th, 1870, at 3 P. M

SUPERIOR COURT.

MARGARET SARAH WALSH, an infant, by JOHN F. WALSH, her guardian,

against

LEWIS A. SAYRE.

June 8, 1870—
Reference, *continued.*

Upon the Referees taking their places, Mr. Croak was about to offer some remarks, Mr. James not being present, when

Mr. SHAFER asked: "Who is the gentleman?"

Mr. CROAK mentioned his name.

Mr. Shafer: Oh! I mean in what capacity you appear here ; as a partner of Mr. James ?

Mr. Croak : Mr. James directed Mr. Walsh to employ somebody to assist him in this matter, he being a young beginner in this country as to the practice. He wished me to post him on the practice, and to enter minutes on the trial, as he never did anything of the kind. If the gentlemen objects to me, I have nothing further to say.

Mr. Shafer : Not at all, not at all ; very glad to see you

Mr. Gage : He is associate counsel in this respect.

Mr. Croak : It may be associate counsel or not ; I would say a mere scrivener.

Mr. Shafer : You were at the circuit ?

Mr. Croak : Yes, sir.

Mr. Shafer : And have been throughout ?

Mr. Croak : Most of it. I will state that Mr. James, having entered his protest, declines to go on further in the case until the matter is decided by the Court whether Dr. Swinburne is a competent Referee in this matter.

Mr. Traphagen : Is that the only ground of the application ?

Mr. Croak : That is all. He is himself engaged in the Schroeder matter at the Tombs, it being set down at half-past one peremptorily.

Mr. Shafer : That he refuses to go on until what ?

Mr. Croak : Until the Court desides—the Superior Court decides—whether Dr. Swinburne is a competent Referee in this matter, on the grounds stated in his protest.

Mr. Traphagen : Is there a stay of proceedings ?

Mr. Croak : No, sir.

Mr. Estes : The only remedy he has, is to go and make a motion to stay the proceedings.

Mr. Croak : That is the step he is going to take.

Judge McKean : It is very evident that the senior counsel needs some one to post him up in this country.

Mr. Shafer : He has been here how long ?

Mr. Gage : Ten years ; I think in 1861 or '62 he was admitted —nine years ago.

Mr. Croak : That is all I have to say.

Mr. Shafer : Is that the ground of his non-attendance ?

Mr. Croak : No, sir ; his engagement in Court.

Mr. Shafer : Do you desire to postpone ?

Mr. Croak : We don't propose to appear until that is decided. I would rather he had made such a statement himself. He said to me, when I called, " I cannot see you to-day, come in to-morrow." I said, " Shall I come in to-morrow ?" and he replied. " it is a reference, and they cannot force me on to trial."

Mr. Traphagen : Is there any ill feeling between you and Mr. James in reference to this matter ?

Mr. Croak : No, none at all, he recommended it, and had a conversation with him before I was called in, and he said he would be very glad to have me in the matter.

Mr. Traphagen : I do not hesitate to say that my own impression is that he has treated his client outrageously, and would say so to Mr. James if he were present, and we have given you more indulgence on that account. We should have closed the case before this.

Mr. Estes : That was expressly one consideration upon which we granted an adjournment the other day. He had gone out, and left you here alone to conduct the case, and upon consultation we concluded to grant an adjournment for that reason, until he should come back.

Mr. Trahhagen : In order not to allow any advantage to be taken, if he is determined not to go on here, if you want to go on and cross-examine the witnesses, you can do so.

Mr. Croak : No, I consider him the senior counsel, and will abide by what he says.

Mr. Traphagen : Then the case is with the other side; you can do what you like.

Mr. Shafer : We have the witnessess here whom we have examined, and we tender them for cross-examination. We have also Dr. Krackowizer, who made the examination on 19th November, 1868, whom we propose to examine on behlaf of the defendant.

Mr. Croak and the guardian for the plaintiff here took their departure, of which fact Mr. Shafer desired this note to be taken.

Mr. Croak made some remark on rising to leave, and

Mr. Gage said : Then I understand him to say that he will remain no longer, and to this no answer was returned.

Mr. Traphagen : I would like to ask if both cases are on trial ?

Judge McKean : I believe it is so understood, that both cases are on trial.

Mr. Traphagen : There was something about the evidence being put in, that if we find for the plaintiff that evidence will be introduced as to expenditures.

Judge McKean : At the first session, when the question was raised, Mr. Shafer being absent, no conclusion was reached, but when the question was subsequently raised, the understanding, as stated by your honor, was made.

Mr. Estes : I got the impression, when the matter came up a day or two ago, that both cases were being considered as tried together, but when they offered some evidence as to special damage, it was objected to and ruled out, but if they were both on trial, it was proper evidence. It was agreed that the principal case was to be tried in the first place.

Judge McKean : At first that was the view, but does not your honor recollect that when you subsequently suggested that, if the cases were on trial, the evidence was admissible ; then it was talked over and agreed that both should be on trial, and, the question of damages should be reserved until the decision of the principal case, and then, if against us, evidence should be introduced in regard to special damages. However that may be, we are to deal with the case as we find it at its present stage, and, after consultation, we have concluded to introduce no more evidence, neither to ask for an adjournment, but we submit the case to your honors for deliberation and for report—for a decision.

Mr. Traphagen : We have, on account of the conduct of the counsel for the plaintiff, considered the matter in some respects, and we have been considering, in the event of our finding or coming to a conclusion, that the report shall be given (if a report), as to what the report shall be entitled. It was a doubt as to whether we can do more than non-suit, and if not that— we could give judgment for the defendant if we felt so disposed —whether that would be a bar to another action.

Mr. SHAFER : There can be no doubt.

Mr. TRAPHAGEN : We have also considered the evidence. The case has been tried with considerable care and attention on the part of the Court, and we have come to the conclusion that, upon all the evidence given, judgment should be granted for for the defendant upon the facts. If you wish to take a report in that manner, you may do so.

Mr. SHAFER : That is the proper form.

Mr. TRAPHAGEN : And you take the responsibility of sustaining it. In this conclusion we refer to the case for damages on the part of the guardian, not for special damages. There is a question as to whether we can dispose of the other case. We cannot say as to that case.

Mr. GAGE : If it please the Court, on the second time of sitting, the question came up, and it was suggested by the counsel for the plaintiff that both cases should be tried together.

Mr. SHAFER : I remember that both were to be tried together, but when evidence was offered in the other case it was excluded, and it was said, in answer to our inquiry, that that case was not on trial. If it had been, that evidence would not have been excluded. It was objected to, and then Mr. Croak said that both were on trial. Then Judge McKean said that something had been said in my absence, and then we conferred together, and it was understood that both should be considered as on trial, until the decision was against us on the main question ; it would be unnecessary to go on for two or three days further.

Messrs. Shafer and Gage then read from the report of the trial as to the understanding of counsel with regard to whether both cases were on trial, when

Mr. TRAPHAGEN said : We do not see that we can dispose of the second case.

Mr. ESTES : It is not before us at all.

Mr. SHAFER : Then we are entitled to the report on the first case, and it leaves us to notice the other case.

Mr. TRAPHAGEN : Yes, you can notice the case.

The report was then drawn by defendant's counsel, and submitted to the Referees.

SUPERIOR COURT

OF THE CITY OF NEW YORK.

MARGARET SARAH WALSH, an infant, by
JOHN F. WALSH, her guardian,

against

LEWIS A. SAYRE. '

The undersigned Referees, duly appointed by this Court, by an order made and entered on the 18th day of May, 1870, and modified on the 28th day of May, 1870; to hear and determine the issues in this case, respectfully report to this Honorable Court, that they have been attended by the respective parties and their respective counsels from time to time, and have heard the evidence and remarks of counsel, and after due deliberation, report as facts :

1st. That on the 27th day of June, 1868, the said John F. Walsh was duly appointed guardian of the plaintiff, for the purposes of this action, as alleged in the complaint.

That the defendant is, and has been, for a great number of years last past, a surgeon, practising in the city of New York.

That the plaintiff, on or about the 2d day of April, 1868, was taken by her mother to the defendant ; he, being such surgeon as aforesaid, to be treated by him for a swelling and injury in the neighborhood of her left hip.

That the cause of said injury was unknown to the mother of the plaintiff, and the defendant, in his capacity as such surgeon, was then consulted by her on behalf of the plaintiff, and was employed, and then undertook such employment as such surgeon, to heal and cure the plaintiff.

2d. That the defendant then and there, after consultation with other surgeons and physicians then in attendance, operated upon the plaintiff for an abscess in the region of the hip, and in making such operation used due and proper care and skill, and large quantities of pus escaped from such abscess after such operation.

3d. That in making said operation he did not puncture the hip joint, nor did he cause the synovial fluid to escape, or to be let out by such operation.

4th. That such operation was performed after a careful and skillful examination of the patient, and in a careful and skillful manner, and the result of the same was to benefit the child.

5th. That the plaintiff has in no way sustained any injury by reason of such operation.

6th. That such operation was necessary to the health of the patient and her recovery.

We further find, as conclusions of law, that the plaintiff has not sustained her alleged cause of action, and that the defendant is entitled to judgment.

Dated, New York City, June 8th, 1870.

> WM. C. TRAPHAGEN,
> BENJAMIN ESTES, } Referees.
> JOHN SWINBURNE,

At a Special Term of the Superior Court of the City of New York, held at the Court House in the City of New York, on the 13th day of June, 1870 :

Present—Hon. JOHN J. FREEDMAN, Justice.

SUPERIOR COURT

OF THE CITY OF NEW YORK.

MARGARET SARAH WALSH, an infant, by JOHN F. WALSH, her guardian,

against

LEWIS A. SAYRE.

Upon reading and filing the affidavit of P. J. Gage, of counsel for defendant, and certificate of Wm. C. Traphagen, John Swinburne, M.D., and Benjamin Estes, Esqs., the Referees appointed herein, and order to show cause, on the part of the plaintiff, or her attorney, why the said defendant should not be granted an extra allowance herein, &c., and due proof of service thereof on the attorney for said plaintiff, and after hearing P. J. Gage, of counsel for defendant, in support of said motion, no one appearing to oppose, it is hereby ordered that said motion be, and the same is hereby granted, and that the defendant be, and he is hereby allowed the sum of five per cent. on the amount claimed by the plaintiff in her complaint against the defendant herein, to wit, the sum of five per cent. on the sum of twenty thousand dollars, as an extra allowance to the defendant herein, in addition to his usual costs.

(A copy). JAMES M. SWEENY, Clerk.

NEW YORK SUPERIOR COURT.

MARGARET SARAH WALSH, an infant, by
    JOHN F. WALSH, her guardian,

against

    LEWIS A. SAYRE.

City and County of New York, *ss.:*

John F. Walsh, the guardian of the plaintiff, being duly sworn says: That on the 18th day of May, 1870, the above entitled action was on the general calendar of the Court for trial, a proposition was made that the same be referred, and the names of William C. Traphagen, Thomas M. North, and John Swinburne, Esqs., were named as such Referees to hear and determine all the issues, and an order to that effect entered, and it was stipulated by and between the attorneys of the respective parties herein, that the same be set down for a hearing, before said Referees on the 2nd day of June, 1870, at 3 o'clock P. M., at the office of said William C. Traphagen, Esq., No. 7 Warren Street; that all parties were in attendance before said Referees, when Thomas M. North, Esq., asked to be excused from serving, as he was a personal friend of Dr. Sayre, the defendant, and that said Sayre was his attending physician and surgeon, and had been for a long time, and that he (said North) was on very intimate and visiting terms with said Sayre and family, and would be prejudiced in the interests of Dr. Sayre. Said North's name was suggested by one of defendant's counsel. Mr. North was then excused, and Mr. Benjamin Estes substituted as a Referee, and the reference then proceeded, testimony taken, and several adjournments were had, when deponent's counsel refused to go on, having heard that Dr. Swinburne, one of the Referees, settled a case in which Dr. Sayre was concerned, involving death, and entered a protest in the words and manner following : "It may be as well to enter my protest against Dr. Swinburne, making it the subject of a motion to the Court. There, I wish to insert in the record that I enter a protest." Dr. Swinburne, in reply to the protest of deponent's counsel, said there was a case of a child that came down from Albany, and had an operation performed, and the case proved fatal, and the family made a good deal of fuss about it. Dr. Sayre asked me if I knew the family, and told me the history of the case. I never saw Dr. Sayre in reference to it. I spoke to the clergyman connected with the diocese. I said here is a case of Dr. Sayre that is perhaps going to make the Doctor trouble, and that was all there was of it. That is all I know of the case.

That said deponent's counsel was overruled, and the said counsel withdrew from the case, still insisting and objecting, under the protest above set forth, that the said Swinburne was incompetent to sit as Referee in this case. Said Swinburne admitted such statements above set forth to be true on the trial. That deponent's counsel refused to go on any further until the question was decided by the Court, and left the case; the Referees refusing to grant his said motion to let the case remain open until that question was decided. That during the absence of deponent's counsel, defendant's counsel insisted upon the trial going on, although deponent's counsel was actually engaged, and disregarding the protest of deponent's said counsel, defendants proceeded to the trial, and obtained a verdict for the defendant.

J. F. WALSH.

Sworn to before me this }
14th June, 1870

SIMON LEVY, Notary Public.

At a Special Term of the Superior Court, held at the Court House, in the City of New York, on the 14th day of June, 1870,

Present—Hon. JOHN J. FREEDMAN, Justice :

MARGARET, SARAH WALSH, an infant, by
   JOHN F. WALSH, her guardian,

against

LEWIS A. SAYRE.

On the annexed affidavit, and on the pleadings and proceedings in this action, let the defendant or his attorney show cause before me, on the 18th day of June, 1870, at 11 o'clock A. M., why John Swinburne, M.D., a Referee in this action, should not be removed as such Referee, and another nominated in his place and stead, on the ground of his, Swinburne's, incompetency, and that a re-hearing of said action be had, and for such other and further relief as may be just, and in the meantime let all proceedings on the part of defendant be stayed.

Dated, June 14th, 1870.

JOHN J. FREEDMAN,

Justice Superior Court.

At the time and place mentioned in the forgoing order, the counsel for the respective parties appeared in Court before his Honor, Justice Freedman.

Mr. James, for the plaintiff, read the affidavit on which the order had been granted, and moved the Court to remove Dr. Swinburne, to appoint another Referee in his stead, and order a re-hearing of the action.

Judge McKean, for the defendant, said : May it please the Court, in the course of my experience I have seen some very remarkable practice, but none so remarkable as this. To show its extraordinary character, permit me to suppose that, instead of being referred, this action had been tried before his Honor, Justice Jones, and a jury, that the trial had proceeded day after day till the plaintiff's testimony was all in, that then, on the eve of an adjournment for the day, the plaintiff's counsel had stated to the Court that he was informed that the defendant (who had practised in this city 28 years), had once lost a patient, and that one of the jurors had, on that occasion, said some word or done some act of kindness towards the defendant—adding, "I shall be able to verify it at the next meeting." Let me suppose, further, that after making this childish charge, the plaintiff's counsel had absented himself from "the next meeting," and utterly abandoned the cause, and after the jury had rendered a verdict against his client, suppose the plaintiff's counsel should move before your Honor to remove the juror referred to, to appoint another in his stead, and grant a new trial—how, I ask—how would your Honor treat such practice as that ? And yet, sir, the case before you is even more remarkable than the one I have supposed. Let us look at it.

This motion is based not alone upon the affidavit read by the learned counsel, but also upon "the pleadings and proceedings in this action." Let us look into the proceedings. The trial had proceeded several days before the Referees, and at length the plaintiff's testimony is all in. The time had now arrived for a stroke of strategy, and the plaintiff's counsel said, " I have received information " &c. *When* did he receive it? That day's session had continued some hours, and the learned counsel had sat at the table all the time. He would not disclose his wonderful "information" until all the plaintiff's testimony was in. He proceeded—"There was some case in which Dr. Sayre performed some operation in which death resulted." What an amazing charge is this! Here is an eminent physician and surgeon, who stands not only in the front rank of his profession, but away up toward the right of the line, and who has practised in this great city from the year 1842 to 1870, and it is gravely charged that in all that long career he has actually lost one patient! Once grim death was more than a match for this man of wonderful skill! And the Court will observe that it was not even insinuated that this one death was caused by any unskillfulness, or carelessness, or fault of Dr. Sayre. On the contrary, the plaintiff's counsel expressly said—" *I do not make any imputation*." What next? Why, Dr. Swinburne, one of the Referees, a physician and surgeon of the highest standing, and a gentleman of the most sensitive honor, is actually and gravely charged with having said or done something of a kindly character in regard to the death of the said patient; and the counsel adds, "I shall be able to verify it at the next meeting." But, doubtless, finding that he could make nothing out of this most childish charge, and having already evinced his disappointment and chagrin at the failure of his witnesses to sustain the allegations of the complaint, the learned counsel for the plaintiff did not appear "at the next meeting," but abandoned the cause !

Without leaving their seats, the Referees found, not only that the plaintiff's cause of action was not made out, but that the defendant's treatment of the plaintiff was skillful, careful, and necessary.

Mr. GAGE, the defendant's attorney of record, then moved before your Honor for an extra allowance of costs; and so extraordinary was the case, that your Honor allowed 5 per cent. on the $20,000 claimed in the complaint—making $1,000—the utmost farthing allowed by the law. And, after all this, the plaintiff's counsel comes here and moves the Court to remove Dr. Swinburne—though the Referees have rendered their report, and, by operation of law, are all discharged—to appoint another in his place, and to order a rehearing of this action. Was there ever a more remarkable proceeding ?

Justice FREEDMAN : There is no such practice. If the plaintiff is aggrieved, the remedy is to bring an appeal. The motion must be denied, with $10 costs.

And thereupon an order was made and entered accordingly.

SUPERIOR COURT

OF THE CITY OF NEW YORK.

MARGARET SARAH WALSH, an infant, by
JOHN F. WALSH, her guardian,

against

LEWIS A. SAYRE.

This cause having been referred to Wm. C. Traphagen, John Swinburne, M.D., and Benjamin Estes, Esq., by this Court, by orders made and entered herein, and bearing date on the 18th and 28th days of May, 1870, the same being hereto annexed, to hear and determine all the issues therein, and the trial thereof having been duly had before said Referees, and their report herein having been filed in the office of the Clerk of this Court, whereby they find in favor of the defendant, Lewis A. Sayre. Now, on motion of P. J. Gage, of counsel for the said defendant, it is hereby adjudged that the complaint herein be dismissed upon the merits of the action, and that Lewis A. Sayre, the defendant, recover of Margaret Sarah Walsh, an infant, by John F. Walsh, her guardian, the plaintiff, the sum of thirteen hundred and fifty-nine dollars and seventy cents ($1,359.70), for his costs and disbursements in this action, and that the said defendant have execution therefor.

JAMES M. SWEENEY, Clerk.

www.ingramcontent.com/pod-product-compliance
Lightning Source LLC
Chambersburg PA
CBHW030842270326
41928CB00007B/1183